# CALIFORNIA

## *WINE COUNTRY*

# COOKING

with Betty Evans

*By the same Author*
CALIFORNIA COOKING WITH BETTY EVANS
VENICE COOKING WITH BETTY EVANS
PARIS COOKING WITH BETTY EVANS
ROME COOKING WITH BETTY EVANS
LONDON COOKING WITH BETTY EVANS
SAN FRANCISCO COOKING WITH BETTY EVANS
HONOLULU HAWAII COOKING WITH BETTY EVANS

# CALIFORNIA
## *WINE COUNTRY*
# COOKING

with Betty Evans

Art by Gordon Evans

SUNFLOWER ❁ INK - CARMEL, CALIFORNIA

# ACKNOWLEDGEMENTS

Very special thanks to Gove and Elizabeth Celio of Liparita Vineyard for caring help; Karen Melander-Magoon of Guenoc Winery for her exceptional hospitality and enthusiasm; Joan and Hal Clark, our Sierra Foothill winery consultants; Steve Hoffmann for perfectionist proof-reading; our son, Bob Evans, for the back cover photo; Ric and Billie Masten for cookbook help and a special friendship over many years; and to M.F.K. Fisher for her continued inspiration.

Library of Congress Catalogue No. 92-064301
ISBN 0-931104-34-3

For Gordon

and our happy times together sharing wine and food

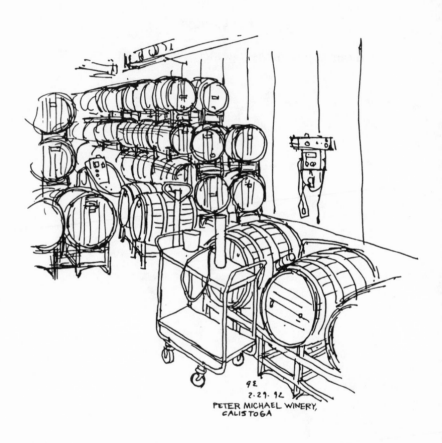

PETER MICHAEL WINERY,
CALISTOGA

SOBON ESTATE MUSEUM,
PLYMOUTH

I've known Betty Evans for more years than either one of us probably cares to remember. I was extremely honored to be asked to write this forward. Betty has always been a big supporter of my partner, Robert Bell and my restaurants, and we have been, in turn, big supporters of her many wonderful cookbooks. I was especially honored to write the forward to this cookbook since it is about a subject very dear to my heart.

Coming to California in 1977 after working for a restaurant group in London, England, I began working in California three days after I arrived, opening a new restaurant. Never having been taught anything about California wines, I decided to do a little self-teaching. Most everything in the wine shops was very average and mostly in jugs.

Having no idea there was even a "wine country" in California, I started putting together a wine list for this new restaurant. My only salvation came in asking several knowledgeable people for help. I was introduced to wines from Robert Mondavi, Rutherford Hill, Parducci, and Sterling. I discovered grapes I had never even heard of, like Chenin Blanc and Chardonnay. I grew up with European wines like Pouilly Fuisse, Chianti and Chateau Latour. I had never tasted California sparkling wines; I only knew Champagne.

It quickly became clear that there was real quality in these California wines. I developed a deep need to go and see Napa Valley and Sonoma County and experience what this California Wine Country was all about. I, like many before me, immediately fell in love with the countryside, the grapes, the people and the lifestyle. As the restaurants which I was involved with grew, so did my interest in wine lists and California wines. I became a California wine groupie. Every time I visit the California Wine Country I feel like I am coming home. The sense of countryside and returning to nature is so calming and relaxing, especially to someone living in Los Angeles. Some of the most exciting evenings I've experienced have been at the homes of winemakers or at restaurants in the wine country where this camaraderie of drinking wine and eating good food come together.

My love for food and my love for wine have made me a natural to enjoy the marvelous region of the California Wine Country which has so expertly blended the two. California cuisine came out of the northern California area. Certainly Alice Waters of Chez Panisse and Jeremiah Towers, then at the Ventana Inn, started the top-quality production of regional cuisine. Can you imagine anything better than Petaluma duck, the cheeses of Sonoma or the cheeses of Laura Chenel, not to mention the wonderful olive oils now produced all over California? Match these with the wondrous selection of California wines. It has all come together here in Betty's book. You cannot doubt that California Wine Country Cooking will introduce you to some of the finest cuisine in the world.

Michael Franks
Owner *Chez Melange Restaurant*
*Redondo Beach, California*

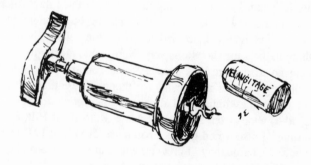

❧ viii ❧

# PREFACE

I had my first taste of wine when I was about seven years old. My father was at that time a sports writer for the Los Angeles Times. He had a colleague named Frankie. Sometimes on a Sunday, Frankie and his wife, Luisa, would invite us over for an Italian Sunday spaghetti dinner. The adults all drank red wine that was made by one of the family cousins and served from an unlabeled green glass jug. I was offered a sip, and thought it tasted like vinegary old grapes.

Often in afternoons my mother, her brother Biddle and sometimes my grandmother enjoyed a sip of sherry. They invited me to have a nip. It made me shudder and wince.

Wine did not become part of my life and dining experiences until I was in my early twenties. My husband Gordon was studying art in Paris on the G.I. Bill. We shared a studio living space with other American student friends. All of us felt that as part of fitting into the French culture, we should drink wine with our meals. Because our incomes were tiny, we bought our wine from Monoprix, a kind of French Woolworth's. We took turns carrying our empty bottles to the store to have them refilled from wine tanks with spigots. The wine choice was red or white from Algeria. It always splashed over the customers' bottles, so this part of the store had a pleasant winey smell. If one of us received some extra money from home or sold a painting, we would buy our wine at Nicholas, a chain of French wine stores. There were many choices, and we liked the Beaujolais or Rosé D'Anjou. I favored the Rosé with its pale rosy color and soft grape flavor.

After school ended, we returned to California. My mom and dad gave us Morrison Wood's cookbook "With a Jug of Wine." I began cooking with wine. It was an exciting revelation and certainly added zest and flavor to ordinary foods. We began drinking California wines. San Antonio Winery had a tasting room in Redondo Beach where we could buy a good table wine in jugs and receive 10¢ for returned bottles.

Our first trip to Napa and Sonoma was to celebrate a wedding anniversary. We met M.F.K. Fisher for the first time, had a picnic with wine at Buena Vista, and took a glider ride in Calistoga. Since that first visit we have returned many times.

The idea for this book came from these visits and our belief that the vineyards of California are among the most beautiful places in the world. We have wandered up and down the state, tasting wine and talking with the proud people involved in the noble business of growing grapes for winemaking. The welcome is warm in every winery from the largest to the smallest. Cooking with wine will certainly improve your cooking, and is fun. Sharing wine with friends and family is surely one of life's finest moments.

Betty Evans
Hermosa Beach, California 1992

HERB GARDEN CAFE CHAMPAGNE, TEMECULA

## COOKING WITH WINE

Cooking with wine is as easy as can be. Wine is used as a flavored liquid; the alcohol evaporates while the food is cooking, and only the magic flavor remains. Wine is usually added at the beginning of the cooking process so that it can mellow. However, it can also have a nice effect when added to the juices in a pan and gently simmered for a few minutes. Wine is used in many marinades for its tenderizing effect.

Never throw away leftover wine. Simply cork it tightly and save it in your refrigerator for cooking. Always use a good quality wine for cooking. It need not be the most expensive, just a wine you would drink yourself. Do not buy those little expensive bottles in the supermarket called "cooking wine." They are inferior, and a sort of scam.

Wine has become recognized as an aid to good health, when used in moderation. Louis Pasteur knew this years ago when he said, "Wine is the most healthful and hygienic of all beverages." M.F.K. Fisher has written, "It seems to me that our three basic needs for food, security and love, are so mixed and mingled and entwined that we cannot straightly think of one without the others ... There is a communion of more than our bodies when bread is broken and wine drunk."

LIPARITA VINEYARD, ANGWIN

ALEXANDER VALLEY
3·21·92

# CHEERS TO MARY FRANCES KENNEDY FISHER

MFK FISHER, GLEN ELLEN

Mary Frances Kennedy Fisher is the eminent goddess of American food writers. Wine and vineyards have always been part of her life. For all of her 83 years, except for her first four years in Michigan, she has lived near vineyards in France, Switzerland and California. For the last two decades she has lived in the small town of Glen Ellen, in the Sonoma Valley. The author of 26 books, she says that wine has always been her favorite beverage. Her approach to wine is honest and without a hint of snobbishness. She will simply tell you that she knows red from white and good from bad. Some years ago she proposed the idea of serving "jug" wine from good vintners at a big local fund raiser for charitable causes. At first there was a bit of a stir, but her idea prevailed, and it was a successful beginning of the promotion of good, reasonably-priced table wines in jugs for wine consumers.

I began my friendship with Mary Frances in 1979 by writing her a letter about her book "Map of Another Town." This is a story about her times in Aix-en-Provence with her two daughters. It was the first book of hers I had read, and I was captivated.

To my happy surprise, she wrote back and asked me about my life. Of course I answered immediately. Our letters continued, and it seemed to me she was a lady of great charm and caring.

In 1981, she invited us to visit her at home on the Bouverie ranch. David Bouverie, an English architect and now a California resident and owner of this large ranch, is a friend of hers, and offered to design a house for her needs.

Mary Frances was waiting for us with wine and little wooden bowls of toasted nuts. She is a tall, handsome woman with a cheerful smile, and was dressed in a purple velour pants suit. Fresh flowers and potted plants filled tables and window sills. She gave us a tour of the house. The back room is for sleeping and working on her writing. The middle room is a comfortable bath room with a big red tub. We sat down in the front room, which is a combination kitchen, dining and sort of living room. There is a large fireplace where she burns oak and madrona wood from the ranch. The windows look out on the high bluish mountains that are part of the Jack London ranch. Mary Frances is a born conversationalist, and we talked about many things: art, food, children, vineyards, diets (which she abhors), France, and the Spanish Civil War. We left feeling fascinated by this enchanting lady.

Since that first visit, we have returned many times to talk and share food and wine with her. She has made us tasty soups, fresh wheat bread, roast chicken, poached salmon, platters of fresh tiny asparagus, and ginger cookies. She has encouraged me with my cookbooks and even purchased them for Christmas gifts. Our children have become her friends and she has sent all of us on our way home with wines, tangerines and cookies.

Once she sent me this favorite recipe of hers for preparing grapes. They can be used as a nibble or a terrific addition to any food.

### PICKLED SEEDLESS GRAPES

Fill one-pint (or smaller) jars with clean seedless grapes, green or preferably 'flame' red. Fill to cover with simple syrup, and cap at once. Serve cold with fish, fowl or cold meats.

To make simple syrup, bring 3 parts granulated sugar and 2 parts white wine vinegar to a full boil, stirring well, and then simmer for 5 minutes.

SOBON ESTATE PICNIC,
PLYMOUTH

# 1. APPETIZERS

SONOMA
12-4-91

## HARASZTHY HUNGARIAN CHEESE SPREAD
### *(Liptauer)*

Agoston Haraszthy was a Hungarian nobleman whose travels led him with his family to Sonoma. In 1857 he began planting grapes on the site of what is now the Buena Vista Vineyard. He was commissioned by the California legislature to gather information about wine producing methods of Europe. From this trip he brought back to Sonoma 100,000 grape cuttings. This pioneering, adventure-seeking man is called "the father of California wine." His palatial home was the scene of many happy social events. This favorite Hungarian dish must have been one of the foods offered on the Hungarian count's table.

*8 oz. cream cheese (at room temperature)*
*1/4 cup butter (at room temperature)*
*1 T minced capers*
*1 T caraway seed*
*3 T minced chives or green onion tops*
*1 T mustard*
*1 T paprika*
*1/4 tsp salt*
*1/4 C sour cream*
*1/2 tsp anchovy paste, or 2 minced*
*anchovies (optional)*

Cream the butter and cream cheese together. Add remaining ingredients and blend. Store in small bowls in the refrigerator. Serve with crackers or small rounds of rye bread. Let the spread sit at room temperature for 20 minutes for easier spreading.

## GENERAL VALLEJO GUACAMOLE

General Mariano Vallejo was a real Renaissance man and one of the first wine producers in Sonoma Valley. He was known for his hospitality and grand entertaining. The General had barbecue parties every week with music and dancing. Among his many interests was introducing new fruit trees to his rancho. It is possible that this included avocado trees, and that some of his 16 daughters might have prepared guacamole for the parties.

*2 ripe avocados, peeled and pitted*
*1 ripe medium-sized unpeeled tomato, cut in tiny pieces*
*2 green onions, minced*
*1 tsp chili powder*
*1 tsp lime or lemon juice*
*salt and pepper to taste*
*1 clove garlic, peeled and finely minced*
*1 small Anaheim or Jalapeno pepper, finely minced (optional)*

Coarsely mash the avocado in a bowl. Leave some tiny lumps for texture. Blend in remaining ingredients and toss gently. Serve with tortilla chips. This will make enough for 4-5. Guacamole is very tasty on toasted sourdough bread or as a topping for grilled meat or fish. It is also popular in California to dip a Carnita (roasted pork piece), speared on a toothpick, in guacamole. See the meat section for a Carnitas recipe.

GENERAL VALLEJO'S HOME, SONOMA

SOBON ESTATE,
PLYMOUTH

## VINELAND STUFFED GRAPE LEAVES
### (Dolmas)

If you live in wine country, little "dolmas" are one of the Spring season's favorite foods to prepare. This recipe has a non-meat filling and is an ideal refreshing beginning to a Spring dinner. Of course, dolmas can be made any time of the year, using preserved bottled leaves.

*40 medium-sized fresh grape leaves (bottled can be used)*
*1 C chopped onion*
*6 T olive oil*
*1/3 C uncooked long-grain rice*
*3/4 C water*
*salt and pepper to taste*
*2 T pine nuts*
*2 T currants*
*1 T fresh chopped mint leaves (optional)*
*1/4 C white wine or water*
*lemon wedges or yogurt for garnish*

If fresh leaves are used, drop them a few at a time in a simmering pot of water. Blanch for 3 minutes. Remove with a slotted spoon and place at once in a bowl of ice water to prevent further cooking. Remove and drain on paper towels. If preserved leaves are used, rinse carefully in cool water and drain. Stems should be snipped-off in either the fresh or preserved leaves.

In a sauce pan, heat 3 T of the oil. Cook onion until limp, add rice and cook just until the grains are glossy, about 2 minutes. Add the water and cover. Cook over a low flame for about 15 minutes. The rice should be tender, but not mushy.

In a small pan, heat 1 T of the oil and brown the pine nuts until just barely golden. Add to rice with the currants, mint (if used) and salt and pepper to taste.

Line the bottom of a heavy 2- or 3-quart casserole with 10 of the leaves. Arrange the remaining leaves, dull side up, on a flat working surface (a bread board works nicely). Snip off any remaining stems.

Place 1 T of the filling in the center of each leaf. Fold the stem end of leaf over the stuffing. Fold left side of leaf toward the center. Repeat with right side. Now, starting at the stem end, roll the leaf into a little sausage-like shape. Do not roll too tightly, as filling will expand slightly.

Stack, with seams down, snugly in the casserole. Sprinkle with remaining olive oil and wine. Cover and simmer over a very low flame for 45 minutes. Uncover, and cool to room temperature. Remove carefully and arrange in an attractive design on a platter. Garnish with lemon wedges. Yogurt may be drizzled over the top, or served on the side. This will make 30 delicious dolmas. They may be refrigerated, but are at their best served at a cool room temperature.

9-14-91
LIPARITA VINEYARD,
ANGWIN

❧ 6 ❧

## HOLIDAY TACO TART

Parties in California are usually casual, and often, on a holiday, a spur-of-the-moment idea. The invitation might be just to come over and bring something for the food table. This tasty concoction of layered Mexican flavors is always popular, and easy to prepare.

*1 17-oz can refried beans*
*1 8-oz carton of sour cream*
*1 pkg of taco seasoning (1-1/4 oz)*
*1 mashed avocado, seasoned with salt and pepper to taste*
*1 7-oz can green chili salsa*
*2 green onions, finely chopped*
*2 C grated cheddar or jack cheese*
*1 2.2-oz can chopped olives, drained*
*2 medium-sized tomatoes, diced*
*cilantro for garnish*
*tortilla chips*

In a 10" or 12" pie pan or bowl, spread out the can of beans. Smooth the top. Spread the sour cream over the beans. Sprinkle half the taco seasoning over the sour cream.

Spread the avocado, then the salsa. Sprinkle onions over the salsa and spread cheese over this. Add the remaining half of the taco seasoning on top of the cheese. Sprinkle the black olives next, followed by the tomatoes.

Cover and refrigerate an hour or more for the flavors to mellow. Before serving, garnish with fresh cilantro. Serve with a sturdy chip that can dip down through the layers without falling apart.

## PICNIC SPINACH PIE

Our family once had a picnic under the pine trees in the hill town of Fiesole, above Florence, where we had come to see the old Roman arena.

We were on a three-month camping trip in Italy and France, and all my cooking was done on a temperamental two-burner camp stove. Any time I saw a tavola caldo (an Italian sort of hot kitchen deli). I would dash in and buy food to supplement our two-burner menu. This day, I bought a gorgeous spinach tart for our picnic lunch, along with a chilled bottle of Soave and some tree-ripened peaches.

When we returned to California, I remembered that tart and decided to make my own version. This recipe comes close. You can cut this pie in small wedges for appetizers, or larger for a picnic.

> *2 10-oz packages frozen chopped spinach*
> *clove fresh garlic, peeled and minced*
> *2 eggs, slightly beaten*
> *1/4 C grated Parmesan cheese*
> *1 tsp nutmeg*
> *salt and pepper to taste*
> *1 C (8 oz.) small curd cottage cheese, or ricotta*
> *1/4 C shelled pine nuts*
> *1 T olive oil*

Cook the spinach according to package directions. Cool and drain, squeezing to remove excess juice. (Fresh spinach may also be used; you will need 3 bunches.) Combine spinach with garlic, eggs, cheese, nutmeg, salt and pepper, and cottage cheese or ricotta. Rub a 10" pie pan with olive oil. Spread the spinach mixture evenly in the pan. Top with the pine nuts and bake at 350° for 20 minutes. Cool on a rack. Serve at room temperature or refrigerate until picnic time.

This tart may also be made in two 9" pans, but will not be as high.

**2. SOUPS**

LIPARITA VINEYARD,
ANGWIN

## WINE LACED SPLIT PEA SOUP

Wine is able to give any simple dish a peppy and tantalizing zap. This classic soup recipe, with just a little wine added, turns into a much improved dish.

Split pea soup was brought from Holland and was popular with pioneer families moving westward to California. Dried peas are rich in vitamins A and B, and provide vegetable protein and minerals. If this recipe is too large, portions can easily be frozen for later use.

*1 pkg. dried split peas (16 oz.)*
*1 ham bone, ham hock, or a few pieces of ham*
*2 stalks of celery, finely chopped*
*1 medium onion, chopped*
*1/2 tsp dried or fresh thyme, crumbled*
*1/2 cup milk or half-and-half*
*1/2 cup dry white wine*
*salt and pepper to taste*

Place the split peas, and seven cups of water, in a soup pot. Add the ham, celery, onion, thyme, salt and pepper. Cover and cook over a low flame until peas are tender, stirring now and then. This will take an hour or more. Remove the ham and cut into small pieces, discarding any bone.

Add the milk (or half-and-half) and wine. Taste for seasoning. Reheat the soup over a very low flame and serve. You can garnish it with some toasted bread cubes or sour cream if desired.

STAVE TOD

## MISSION ALBONDIGAS SOUP

Albondigas soup is a legacy from California's mission days. Missions always had vineyards for their sacramental wine. This soup, with its combination of Spanish and Mexican flavors, is a wonderful choice for a soup dinner. Serve it with hot tortillas, a green salad and your favorite red wine.

*1 T oil*
*1 onion, finely chopped*
*1 clove garlic, minced*
*1 slice white bread*
*1 egg, slightly beaten*
*1 lb ground lean beef, or a combination*
*    of pork and beef*
*1/2 tsp oregano*
*1/2 cup white or yellow corn meal*
*salt and pepper to taste*
*1 fresh green Anaheim chile, seeded and finely chopped*
*2 qts of chicken or beef stock*
*    (homemade or canned)*
*1 8-oz. can tomato sauce*

Heat the oil in a frying pan. Lightly brown the garlic and onion. Break the bread into small pieces and mix with the beaten egg to make a smooth consistency. Add to the meat, along with the cooked onion and garlic, oregano, corn meal, chile, salt and pepper. Form the mixture into small meatballs about the size of a walnut.

Heat the stock with the tomato sauce. Drop the meatballs into the soup. Cook uncovered over a low flame for 25 minutes. To serve, place 3 meatballs in each soup bowl and fill with the broth. This will serve 6. Garnish with a few cilantro leaves if desired. Leftover meatballs make a tasty sandwich!

CASK SPIGOT

## NAPA VALLEY MINESTRONE

Among the Italian communities in Napa Valley, minestrone has always been a favorite soup. This is a basic recipe. Italian kitchens are always very inventive, and each cook will add a little more of this or that to the pot. Use your own imagination, and have fun!

*3 qts. water*
*1 onion, chopped*
*1 or 2 lbs beef shank bones, or any other soup bone*
*3 stalks celery, diced*
*1 cup dried Northern or Navy white beans*
*1 cup dried red kidney beans*
*1 14-1/2 oz. can whole tomatoes*
*2 cloves garlic, minced*
*1 tsp dried or fresh thyme*
*2 medium zucchini, diced*
*1 10-oz. pkg frozen peas*
*1 10-oz. pkg frozen lima beans*
*1 15-oz can garbanzo beans*
*1/2 cup spaghetti (broken in 1-inch lengths)*
*salt and pepper to taste*
*1 cup white or red wine*
*Parmesan cheese and minced parsley for garnish*

In a large soup pot put the water, onion, garlic, celery, bone, beans, tomatoes, thyme, salt and pepper. Break up the tomatoes if they are too large. Simmer, covered, until the beans are tender, about one hour. Add zucchini, peas, limas, garbanzos and spaghetti; cook, uncovered, until the vegetables are tender (about 15 minutes). This is a thick soup; if you want it thinner, add additional wine or other liquid. Before serving, discard the bone, mince any meat from the bone and return it to the soup. Garnish with Parmesan and parsley. This will serve 10, and any leftover soup can be frozen.

HOOP DRIVER

## WINE FLAVORED ONION SOUP

My first taste of onion soup was in Paris, at one of the little cafes that lined the streets leading to Les Halles, the enormous food market. It was around three on a very cold February morning. I had come to the market to buy various ingredients for a cassoulet, which was to be the main dish for a Mardi Gras party.

The cafe was crowded with market porters, super-strong men who can easily carry a 400-pound calf over their shoulders. These men firmly believe that onion soup and a glass of wine will fortify their strength for this heavy labor.

Onion soup is also recommended for curing hangovers. It was the custom for Paris revelers to stop for a bowl of soup after an evening of parties. Porters and Parisians in evening dress sat side by side, enjoying their soup. In the name of progress, the market has now been moved to the outskirts of the city. A few of the original popular cafes remain, but the atmosphere is not the same, unfortunately.

Onion soup is easy to prepare at home with this recipe. The success of this soup lies in the slow cooking of the onions.

*4 T butter*
*6 medium onions, peeled and finely sliced*
*1 T flour*
*2 quarts chicken or beef stock or broth*
*   (canned or homemade)*
*salt and pepper to taste*
*1 cup dry white wine*

Melt the butter in a soup pot. Add the sliced onions. Stir, cover and simmer for twenty minutes, stirring occasionally. Stir in salt, pepper and flour. Add stock and wine, then simmer, uncovered, for 40 minutes. This will serve 6. Hot sourdough bread can be served with the soup. Freshly grated Parmesan cheese may be sprinkled on the top.

SC
TRA VIGNE
ST. HELENA
3-19-92

## VENETIAN CELERY, RICE AND SAUSAGE SOUP

Grape growing places are thought of as sunny and hot. In winter, however, they are very cold. The vines are pruned and leafless, resting before the early spring growth. This is the season for wine country soup dinners and this delicious Venetian soup.

*2 T butter or olive oil*
*1 medium onion, chopped*
*2 Italian sausages (about 1/2 lb, either hot or sweet)*
*5 cups chicken broth*
*1 cup dry white wine*
*1-1/2 cups diced celery*
*salt and pepper to taste*
*1/2 cup uncooked short-grain rice*
*1/4 cup Parmesan cheese,*
    *and 2 T minced parsley, for garnish*

In a soup pot, melt the butter (or oil), and add the onion. Remove casing from sausage; crumble in small pieces and add to the onion. Stir-fry together a few minutes, just until the onion becomes limp. Add broth and wine, with salt and pepper to taste. Now add the celery. Cover and simmer for 30 minutes. Remove cover, add rice, and simmer an additional 20 minutes. Serve garnished with cheese and parsley. This will serve 4-5.

# RUNNING STREAM WATERCRESS SOUP

Watercress soup is both pretty and perfect for a luncheon. Watercress grows freely along many California streams. It is used in salads and is a popular garnish. It gives soup a nice nip and the green flecks of cress make the soup attractive.

*1 lb potatoes, peeled and sliced in 1 inch slices*
*41/2 cups water*
*1 onion, peeled and diced*
*1 cup milk (or half-and-half)*
*salt and pepper to taste*
*1/4 cup dry white wine*
*1 bunch watercress*
*dash nutmeg (optional)*

Combine potatoes, onion, water, salt and pepper in a soup pot. Cover and simmer for 40 minutes or until the potatoes are very tender.

Remove the pot from the stove and, using a fork, break up the potatoes until you have a crumbly texture. Do not use a blender or food processor as this will produce a baby food mixture.

Wash the watercress, chop into 1/2" pieces, and add to the soup, along

CHATEAU ST. JEAN,
KENWOOD
3- 20- 92

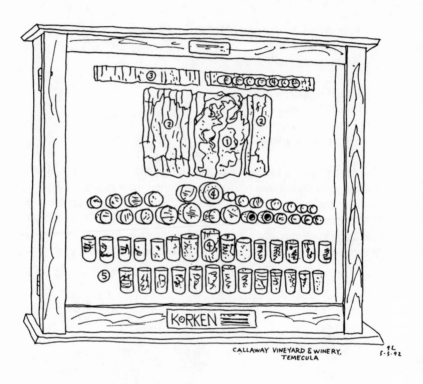

KORKEN

CALLAWAY VINEYARD & WINERY,
TEMECULA

Mustards

EN. GRILL · WINE · BEER · CONDIMENTS ESPRESSO

MUSTARDS, 2·28·92
NAPA

# 3. FISH

HOP KILN WINERY
HEALDSBURG

## SPRING SALMON WITH CUCUMBER SAUCE

Tender new spring grape buds are pale green, with a pinkish tinge. They are a beautiful promise of the coming summer's grape harvest. The delicate pink color of salmon combined with cucumber makes a pleasant dinner for a spring evening.

*4 serving size pieces of salmon*
  *(either filets or steaks; about 3 to 3-1/2 lbs.)*
*1/4 cup butter*
*juice of 1 medium lemon*
*1/4 cup dry white wine*
*1 cucumber*
*salt and pepper to taste*
*parsley for garnish*

Melt the butter. Mix with the lemon juice, salt, pepper and white wine. Place the salmon in a shallow baking dish that will fit the fish pieces. Pour the seasoned liquid over it. Cover with foil. Bake at 350° for 25 minutes or until salmon is cooked. It will be pink and flake easily.

While the salmon is cooking, peel the cucumber. Remove the seeds and dice into quarter-inch cubes. Cook the cubes 5 minutes in simmering salted water. Drain immediately and set aside.

To serve, place each salmon steak on a warmed place. Pour the juices from the pan over the salmon servings. Strew with the cucumber, and garnish with some finely minced parsley. Boiled new buttered potatoes are a good accompaniment. This will serve 4.

# SEA BASS IN AN EASY WINE SAUCE

White wine adds a magic flavor touch to fish cooking. This method of marinating and then completing the cooking with the marinade is a popular California wine country cooking technique. This recipe is usually served hot; however, on hot summer days it may be chilled and served on a bed of fresh grape leaves.

> 2-1/2 lbs fresh sea bass, halibut or any firm fish
> 1/4 cup olive oil
> juice from one medium lemon
> 2 cloves fresh garlic, peeled and minced
> salt and pepper to taste
> 1 bay leaf (fresh or dried), crumbled in tiny pieces
> flour
> 1/2 cup white wine
> 2 T butter and 2 T olive oil for frying
> parsley and lemon wedges for garnish

Mix the olive oil, lemon, garlic, salt, pepper and bay leaf together. Cut the fish in 4 serving pieces. Place the fish in a shallow glass or china dish and cover with the marinade. Cover and marinate in a cool place for one hour, turning once during this time.

Remove the fish from the marinade, reserving marinade. Pat dry with paper towels. Dust with flour on both sides. Fry one side until golden brown. Turn and fry the remaining side. Lower the flame and add the marinade and wine. Cover and cook until the fish is done (about 10 minutes, depending on the fish). Serve with the pan wine sauce. Garnish with lemon wedges and minced parsley. This will serve 4.

END OF
HARVEST
LA JOTA, ANGWIN

## PARTY FISH KEBABS

There is a lot of outdoor cooking among the wine growers. The slightest excuse is reason for a party: weather, a birthday, a friend's visit, or any happy event! These kebabs are a good choice for the main dish. They are at their best cooked on a barbecue; however, if the day should turn cool, they may be done in an inside broiler. Rice, seasonal vegetables and a tomato salad will complete the party. Chilled Chardonnay or Sauvignon Blanc are good wine choices.

*2 lbs. fresh swordfish or shark*
*1/4 cup olive oil*
*juice from one fresh medium lemon*
*1/4 cup dry white wine*
*1/2 tsp paprika*
*2 T onion juice (made by rubbing a raw onion over a grater)*
*salt and pepper to taste*
*20 bay leaves (fresh preferred)*

Cut the fish into one-inch cubes. Combine remaining ingredients (except bay leaves) in a bowl. Place the fish in the marinade and refrigerate for 2-3 hours.

To prepare for the barbecue, remove the fish from the marinade. Thread on metal skewers, placing an occasional bay leaf between the fish cubes. Barbecue or broil, keeping the fish about 5 inches from the fire. Baste with marinade while turning skewers so that fish is lightly browned on all sides. Serve by sliding fish off the skewer and onto a bed of rice. This will serve 4, but the recipe can easily be increased for parties.

## SOLE WITH FRESH GRAPES

August Escoffier, the master French chef, combined grapes with sole in honor of the French opera "Veronique." This combination worked very well, and California vintners use this easy version of the classic French recipe.

> *1 lb. fresh filet of sole, sliced*
> *flour*
> *salt and pepper to taste*
> *5-6 T butter*
> *1/2 cup white wine*
> *about 32 white seedless grapes, peeled (Thompsons work well)*

Dust the sole pieces with flour. Heat the butter in a frying pan. As soon as the butter is hot, but before it browns, gently fry each filet on both sides until golden brown. Season with salt and pepper and remove to a warm platter. You may have to cook the fish in two batches, so the amount of butter for frying may need to be increased.

Add the wine and grapes to the butter in the pan. I prefer the grapes peeled, if you have the time. Peeling grapes can be relaxing and adds class to this recipe.

Pour the sauce over the cooked sole. The dish may be garnished with fresh grape leaves and little bunches of grapes. This will serve 3. Be sure to include a bottle of chilled white Sauvignon Blanc wine with your Veronique supper!

## VALLEY TROUT WITH MUSHROOMS

Streams, rivers and peaceful lakes add to the beauty of the grape growing valleys of California. These waters are plentiful with trout. There is also a flourishing trout farm industry up and down the state.

Trout has always been the favorite fresh fish in California. When Lilly Langtry, "the Jersey Lily" and her sweetheart Freddie Gebhart arrived at their newly purchased ranch in Guenoc valley (now the home of the Guenoc winery), fresh trout was part of the dinner.

Frying is one of the easiest ways to prepare trout, and garnished with mushrooms, it makes a quick, delicious meal.

*4 fresh or defrosted trout (about 3/4 lb each)*
*1/2 cup butter (1 4-oz cube)*
*1/3 cup cooking oil*
*flour for dusting*
*salt and pepper to taste*
*fresh lemon wedges and parsley for garnish*
*1/2 lb. fresh mushrooms, washed and sliced*

Pat the trout dry with a paper towel. Dust with flour. Heat one half of the cube of butter with the oil in a large frying pay. Add the fish to the pan. Brown well on both sides, seasoning with salt and pepper. This will take 5-6 minutes for each side.

Melt the remaining butter in another frying pan, add mushrooms and gently fry just until light brown. Sprinkle with a little salt and pepper.

When the trout is done, place on warmed plates, sprinkle with mushrooms and minced parsley. Add lemon wedges. Boiled new potatoes are the traditional accompaniment. This will serve 4. Chilled Chardonnay is a good wine choice for trout.

END OF HARVEST
LA JOTA, ANGWIN

# 4. POULTRY

# NAPA CHICKEN CACCIATORA

This recipe, brought to Napa by Italian settlers in the valley, continues to be in use in homes and restaurants. It is often served by vintners' families on Sundays with their favorite pasta. Rabbit is sometimes substituted for chicken.

*1 3-4 lb. chicken, cut up, or chicken parts*
*1/2 cup flour*
*1/2 to 3/4 cup olive oil*
*1 onion, chopped*
*2 cloves garlic, minced*
*1 red or green bell pepper, chopped*
*1/2 tsp thyme, fresh or dried*
*1/2 tsp oregano, dried or fresh*
*salt and pepper to taste*
*3/4 cup dry white wine*
*1/4 cup red or white wine vinegar*
*1 cup sliced fresh mushrooms*
*1/4 cup chopped olives*
*2 cups canned whole tomatoes, or peeled fresh*

I find the simplest way to coat chicken with flour is the old-fashioned way: put some flour in a paper bag, add the chicken, and shake to coat. Heat the oil in a large frying pan. Brown the chicken on both sides (this may have to be done in two batches). Remove the chicken. Add the onion and garlic to the same pan, scraping up bits from chicken frying. Fry just until limp. Stir in the wine, vinegar, tomatoes and seasonings, breaking up any large pieces of tomatoes. Give a good stir. Add the pepper, mushrooms, olives and chicken. Cover the pan and simmer until the chicken is tender (about 45 minutes). This dish may also be baked, in a three- or four-quart pan, at 350° for 45 minutes.

Serve to 4, with pasta and plenty of crusty Italian bread, and either red or white wine.

ROBERT MONDAVI, OAKVILLE
3-26-92

V. SATTUI WINERY.
ST. HELENA

## CHICKEN IN RED WINE SAUCE
### *(Coq au vin)*

Red wine is what makes this dish so flavorful and lusty, in contrast to delicate white wine poultry recipes. The chicken pieces are slowly baked in the red wine sauce, and the flavor will improve if it's made a day ahead. This is a perfect dish for a party, served with boiled potatoes to soak up the juices and a fresh green salad. A Merlot or burgundy is a good choice for the cooking and may also be served with the dinner.

> *2 chickens, about 3 lbs each, cut in serving pieces*
> *flour for coating the chicken*
> *6 T butter plus 2 T cooking oil*
> *1/4 lb. diced ham (or lean uncooked bacon)*
> *1/4 lb. fresh mushrooms, sliced*
> *18 small boiling onions, peeled*
> *1 tsp thyme, dried or fresh*
> *salt and pepper to taste*
> *1 bay leaf*
> *1/4 cup brandy or cognac*
> *4 cups dry red wine, plus more if needed*

Pat the chicken dry and dredge in the flour. Heat the butter and oil in a large oven casserole. Add the chicken pieces and lightly brown a few at a time, adding more butter or oil if necessary. Return all pieces to the pot and add remaining ingredients except the wine and brandy.

Pour the brandy or cognac over the chicken and light with a match. Do not get your face too close to the flame. When the flame dies out, add the wine. Stir and cover casserole. Bake in a 325° oven for an hour and a half, or until chicken is tender. Stir now and then during the baking, adding more wine if necessary. This will serve 8.

## FIESTA CHICKEN ENCHILADAS

Enchiladas are a California heritage from the mission and rancho days. The tradition continues in the wine country today. Enchiladas can be made ahead in large quantities, which makes this dish an ideal choice for any "fiesta" celebration. This recipe can be used for anything from wedding receptions to a late brunch menu.

*12 medium-sized flour or corn tortillas*
*2 cooked chicken breasts*
*1 8-oz pkg. cream cheese (room temperature)*
*6 green onions, minced*
*2 cups grated Jack cheese*
*1 4-oz can diced green chiles*
*1 8-oz can tomato sauce*
*1 cup sour cream*
*oil for frying if corn tortillas are used*
*salt and pepper to taste*
*1 tsp chili powder*
*cilantro, avocado slices and olives for garnish (optional)*

Bone, skin and shred the chicken breasts in long pieces (about 2-1/2 inches long). Cream the cheese with a wooden spoon until smooth. Mix in the chicken, green onions, salt, pepper, and half of the diced chiles. Now blend in one cup of the Jack cheese. This is the filling, and can easily be made ahead.

If flour tortillas are used, simply heat until limp on a griddle or frying pan. If corn tortillas are used, heat a little oil and fry the tortillas until limp. Fill each tortilla with a heaping tablespoon of the filling. Roll the tortilla and place seam down in a lightly greased baking pan.

Mix the sour cream with the tomato sauce, chili powder and remaining diced chiles. Spoon over tortillas. Sprinkle with the remaining cheese. Bake at 325° for 20 minutes, uncovered. They should be hot, with the cheese melted. Do not overcook as the tortillas will become mushy. Garnish as desired. Pale green avocado slices arranged on the top will look lovely.

# DINNER PARTY ROMAN CHICKEN

When we lived in Rome, there was a little trattoria in our Piazza del Popolo neighborhood. At lunchtime, it was always crowded with local people who would meet for the long noon meal. This ceremony of dining in courses, with long Italian conversations and much facial and hand gesturing, lasted about two hours. We were always greeted with a warm and friendly "Buon Giorno!"

If our youngest daughter Jeanne was with us, she was the star, with a "Ciao Bella!" hello and a gift banana from the fresh fruit tray.

One of my favorite things from the menu was this simple Roman chicken combination. In Rome, it is served with a carafe of one of the refreshing white wines from the nearby Alban hills. The friendly cook, Leonardo, shared this recipe with me. It is ideal for a party; you can make it ahead of time, and heat it while your guests enjoy wine and antipasto.

> *4 whole chicken breasts, boned and skinless (about 3 lbs.)*
> *8 thin slices of prosciutto*
> *1/4 lb. fontina, Swiss, or Jack cheese, sliced thin*
> *flour*
> *1 T sage (minced if fresh; crushed if dried)*
> *salt and pepper to taste*
> *Parmesan cheese*
> *1/2 cup white wine*
> *3 T olive oil and 3 T butter, plus olive oil for baking pan*

Cut the breasts in two so you have 8 pieces. Place them between sheets of waxed paper. Flatten with a meat pounder or the bottom of a heavy bottle. Sprinkle with salt and pepper and dust with flour.

In a frying pan, heat the butter and oil. Lightly brown the chicken on each side. This will take only a few minutes; if chicken breasts are overcooked they become dry.

In a large baking pan, spread a thin layer of olive oil. Place the pieces of chicken in the pan. Lay a piece of prosciutto on each piece. Top with a cheese slice, and sprinkle the sage over all. Dribble the wine over the chicken, and sprinkle with Parmesan cheese. Cover with foil and bake in a 300° oven for 20 minutes. If you have made this dish ahead and it is cold, add about 10 more minutes warming time. Serve with pasta, green salad, crusty bread and chilled Chenin Blanc or Chardonnay. This will serve 4.

# NANA'S GUMBO

Gumbo is a unique stew from Louisiana. This classic American dish has become popular with California chefs up and down the state. It is fun to make and can vary with each cook's favorite ingredients.

For me, gumbo is a wonderful sentimental dish. It was often made by my grandmother, whom we called "Nana." She was born on a Louisiana plantation. In the family kitchen there was always ham from the smokehouse, fresh chickens, and okra from the garden. Each day street vendors would come by with fresh shrimp, oysters and crabs. The cook would make her choice of the seafood and combine with the plantation ingredients in a big pot to cook slowly. Gumbo was always served with large bowls of freshly-cooked rice.

My mother continued the gumbo tradition for family gatherings and parties. She would make it a day ahead so the flavors could "mellow." You might serve a rosé wine with this marvelous creation.

*1 whole chicken, cut up, or parts (about 3 lbs)*
*1 large onion, chopped*
*1 cup diced ham*
*1/4 cup cooking oil (peanut recommended)*
*1 28-oz. can solid pack tomatoes*
*1/2 cup dry white wine*
*1 10-oz pkg of frozen okra, or 1-1/2 cups fresh, sliced*
*salt and pepper to taste*
*1 lb shrimp, peeled and deveined*
   *(or 1 lb. crab, or 12 medium-sized fresh oysters, shucked)*

Heat the oil in a frying pan. Brown the chicken pieces, ham and onion all together. The chicken is just lightly fried to seal in the juices, so this procedure is sort of a light, quick stir-fry. Put the chicken and pan juices in a large pot; add tomatoes, wine, salt, and pepper. Cover and cook until the chicken is tender, about 45 minutes. Remove chicken, and when cool enough to handle, remove meat from bone. Return to pot with okra and cook, uncovered, for an additional 15 minutes, adding seafood the last 7 minutes. My nana and mother did not use Filé powder as they felt the okra was enough thickening. This will serve 6.

YOSEMITE

# 5. MEAT DISHES

## WINE BRAISED BEEF ROAST

There are many French influences in wine country recipes. Wine is unsurpassed in slow cooking, as in this version of a Boeuf à la mode (which simply means, in English, "Fashionable Beef"). Any leftovers can be used in a sandwich, or julienned for a salad.

Although carrots, potatoes and onions are the traditional vegetables, there is no reason why you can't use any seasonal vegetable. Either rice or potatoes can be served with the beef. Mashed potatoes are excellent with the marvelous winey juices.

> *1 4-5 lb. beef roast (rump, shoulder or round)*
> *4 T butter (or bacon drippings)*
> *3 T flour*
> *2-3 cups of dry red wine*
> *1 cup stock (or water)*
> *3 slices of uncooked bacon, diced*
> *salt and pepper to taste*
> *1/4 tsp thyme, dried or fresh*
> *2 bay leaves*
> *3 onions, chopped*
> *6 carrots, peeled and trimmed*

Melt the butter in a heavy oven casserole. Brown the meat on both sides. Remove from the pot and set aside. Stir in the wine and stock, and stir around to blend. Add bacon, salt, pepper, bay leaves, thyme and onions. Place the meat back in the pan. Cover and cook in a 325° oven for 2 hours. Check now and then to make sure there is enough liquid; if not, add additional wine. Add carrots after one hour. Small potatoes may be added the last 30 minutes. This will serve 6. Slice the roast and serve with the vegetables. Garnish each plate with some snipped fresh parsley.

# CLASSIC BEEF BURGUNDY

There is nothing more typical of Wine Country cooking than a simple beef stew cooked in wine. This version is from France, and is a favorite on those nippy winter days in California vineyards.

*2 lbs round, chuck or stewing beef, cut in 1-1/2" cubes*
*3 T oil (or bacon drippings)*
*4 medium white onions, peeled and sliced*
*2 T flour*
*1 T thyme*
*2 cups Burgundy or other dry red wine*
*1-1/2 cups beef stock, canned beef bouillon or water*
*salt and pepper to taste*
*1/2 lb. fresh mushrooms, sliced*
*parsley for garnish*

Heat the oil or drippings in a heavy stew pot. Cook the onions just until limp. Remove with a slotted spoon and set aside. Lightly brown the beef cubes in the same oil, adding additional if needed. When the meat is browned, stir in the flour and blend. Add the liquid and wine. Season with thyme, salt and pepper. Cover and bake at 325° for about two hours. Stir now and then, and add additional wine if liquid is low. This may also be simmered on top of the stove if desired. Add mushrooms the last 30 minutes of cooking. This will serve 4. I like to serve rice with beef burgundy, but boiled potatoes or buttered noodles may also be used. A green salad and sturdy chunky bread to dip in the wondrous juices will complete the meal. Of course, Burgundy is the wine choice!

SOBON ESTATE,
PLYMOUTH
4-24-92

# YOSEMITE CAMPFIRE CHILI

There aren't any vineyards in Yosemite, but it is certainly one of the most beautiful places in the state to enjoy wine. This is made especially easy when, in the late fall, leading winemakers of California meet at the Ahwanee Hotel for a "Yosemite Vintners' Holiday." In the Great Lounge of this historic hotel, with its massive fireplaces crackling, you can attend informative talks with top vintners and taste premium wines.

Following these sessions there are dinners in the incomparable dining room. In this 130-foot-long room, with its high ceilings, you will experience one of the most dramatic dining rooms in the world. The view from the massive windows is a nature wonderland.

Our family has camped in the wondrous radiant Yosemite valley, and sipped wine around a campfire while we prepared our chili dinner. Sometimes I have frozen this chili at home and carried it to the park in our ice chest.

Information about these Vintners' Holidays is available by calling (209) 454-2020, or writing to Holidays, 5411 East Home Ave., Fresno, CA 93727.

*4 T vegetable oil*
*2 large onions, finely chopped*
*2 cloves garlic, finely chopped*
*2 Anaheim chiles, finely chopped*
*2 lbs beef boneless chuck or round, cut in about half-inch cubes*
*4 T chili powder*
*1 tsp cumin (seeds or ground)*
*1 28-oz can solid pack tomatoes*
*2 cups liquid (wine, beer, broth or water)*
*salt and pepper to taste*

Heat oil in a 3-4 quart stew pot. Add onions, garlic and chiles. Stir until ingredients are limp. Add beef with seasonings and stir until blended. Add the canned tomatoes, breaking up any large pieces. Add liquid, salt and pepper. Cover and cook over a low flame or in oven (325°) for one hour or until the meat is tender, stirring now and then. Canned drained beans may be added if desired.

The chili can be served with bowls of sour cream, dried red peppers, grated cheese, chopped onions and shredded lettuce for garnishes. This will serve 5. Warmed tortillas and Zinfandel wine will add to the enjoyment of campfire chili.

TOPOLOS
·RUSSIAN RIVER VINEYARDS,
FORESTVILLE

## RUSSIAN RIVER CABBAGE ROLLS

Two-lane roads meander among oak-covered hills along the Russian River. This is the site of many fine wineries, and it is a joy to travel in this peaceful countryside. Russians, who had come in pursuit of the sea otter, were the first settlers in this Northern Sonoma area. Their colony was called Rossiya, which is now the Fort Ross state historical park.

The Russians grew grape cuttings brought from the Black Sea. They also grew cabbages, from which they made this favorite Russian dish.

*1 large head of cabbage*
*1 lb. lean ground beef*
*1 T bacon drippings (or vegetable oil)*
*1 medium onion, chopped*
*1 clove garlic, minced*
*2 T parsley*
*salt and pepper to taste*
*juice of 1/2 lemon*
*1 egg*
*4 T butter*
*1 T flour*
*1 cup solid pack tomatoes*
*1/2 cup dry red wine*
*1 cup sour cream*

Heat water in a pot large enough to hold the head of cabbage. When it is boiling, add the head of cabbage. Cover and simmer for 10 minutes. Drain the cabbage and, when cool enough to handle, remove 12 of the largest leaves. The remainder of the cabbage can be used for soup.

In a frying pan, melt the drippings (or oil). Saute the onion and garlic until limp. In a bowl, mix the beef with salt, pepper, parsley, lemon juice, egg and cooked onion and garlic. Blend together. This mixture is your stuffing.

Fill each leaf with a heaping tablespoon of the stuffing. Roll up in the leaf, using a toothpick to hold together if necessary.

Melt the butter in a frying pan. Brown the rolls lightly. Carefully place the rolls in a flat baking dish. To the juice remaining in the pan, blend in the flour. Stir to make a smooth paste. Add the tomatoes, wine and sour cream. Cook a minute to blend. Pour sauce over rolls. Cover and bake at 325° for 45 minutes. Hot steamed rice or mashed potatoes may be served with this Russian treat.

DOMAINE MICHEL
12-3-91 HEALDSBURG

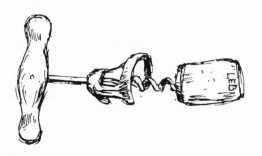

## ROMAN PICNIC FLAT MEATBALLS WITH LEMON
### *(Polpette alla limone)*

One of my favorite picnic spots in the Russian River area is the Hop Kiln Winery. This is a California landmark, built over 100 years ago. Hops were grown in this area for breweries at the beginning of the century. Some of the original equipment is on display, with fascinating photos of this time.

There are picnic tables by the tranquil duck pond, with another picnic spot under a spreading Kadota fig tree planted in 1880. These Roman flavored patties make a terrific picnic lunch. Serve with sourdough bread, olives, fresh fruit and a bottle of Hop Kiln wine or champagne.

*1 lb. lean ground beef*
*1 egg*
*1/4 cup red or white wine*
*1 slice of white bread (any kind)*
*2 tsp minced fresh parsley*
*salt and pepper to taste*
*grated rind of 1 medium lemon*
*1 clove of garlic, minced*
*olive oil for frying*
*lemon wedges and minced parsley for garnish*

Lightly beat the egg in a medium-sized bowl. Stir in the wine. Crumble the bread into this mixture and let stand a few minutes to absorb the liquid. Add the remaining ingredients to the bowl and blend together. Form the meat into flat cakes about 1/2" high and 2-1/2" in diameter. Heat enough olive oil in the pan to permit even frying (a non-stick pan works well). Fry meat patties on each side until golden brown. They may be eaten hot or cold. Garnish with lemon wedges or parsley. This will make 6 cakes.

# CARNITAS WITH SALSA

*Carnitas* in Spanish simply means little pieces of crispy meat. You can use this recipe for a casual dinner, part of a Mexican feast, or as a snappy appetizer. Carnitas baked in the oven is an easy way to prepare this tasty California Mexican heritage dish. Serve with a bowl of salsa or guacamole.

> *3 lbs of pork shoulder or other cut of pork*
> *salt and pepper to taste*
> *2 T chili powder*
> *1 T cumin seed or powder*
> *cilantro and lime wedges for garnish (optional)*

Cut the pork into 1-1/2" cubes. Pork for this dish should have some fat as this produces the crispy character of the dish. Place the pork cubes on a shallow, lightly greased baking pan. Sprinkle the pork with salt, pepper, chili and cumin. Bake in a 325° oven for one hour, stirring now and then. Drain and serve from a warmed platter. The drained fat may be used for refried beans.

## SALSA

There are many salsa recipes. This will provide a guide; more or less of any ingredient may be used according to your taste. Remember to use caution when you use chiles. Wash your hands well after peeling chiles, and never rub your eyes while preparing chiles.

> *3 medium tomatoes, peeled and chopped*
> *1 onion, peeled and chopped*
> *1 clove garlic, peeled and chopped*
> *2 Anaheim chiles, chopped finely*
> *1 tsp vinegar or lime juice*
> *2 T fresh minced cilantro*

Mix all together and let stand about one half hour for flavors to mellow. Jalapeno or Serrano chiles may be added for extra hotness.

# CHOUCROUTE GARNI
## *(Sauerkraut garnished with sausages and meats)*

When I was growing up, one of my uncles used to open a can of sauerkraut, dump it in a pot to warm, and then proceed to eat it. I thought it smelled awful and tasted worse. When I lived in Paris, I was served "choucroute" by a young French lady who had married one of our friends. I loved every bite and asked how it was cooked. "With white wine" was her answer. White wine will turn sauerkraut into a delicious taste treat. While beer is often served with this dish, many in California and France prefer a chilled white wine.

*1 27-oz can sauerkraut (or 3-4 cups deli sauerkraut)*
*4 slices bacon*
*1 tsp caraway seeds*
*6 juniper berries*
*salt and pepper to taste*
*2 cups dry white wine (plus a little more if needed)*
*1 cup water or stock*
*sausages of your choice -*
  *Bratwurst, Knackwurst, Frankfurter, etc*
*pork chops (smoked is a good choice)*
*small boiled potatoes*

Place the sauerkraut in a strainer. Run cold water over it to wash away the curing juices. Drain thoroughly. Place the bacon on the bottom of a heavy 3-4 quart casserole. Place the sauerkraut on top of the bacon. Cover with seeds, berries, salt, pepper, wine, and stock. Cover and bake in a 325° oven for one hour. Remove cover and add more liquid if needed. Add sausages. This will serve 4 so it depends on how hungry your diners are as to the amount of sausages needed. One pork chop apiece is usually enough, and may be omitted if you prefer just sausages. Potatoes may be peeled and either cooked separately or added to the pot. Usually 2 small potatoes are enough for each portion.

Cover and cook an additional 30 minutes. Serve to 4, with assorted mustards. It is easy to double the recipe for a party and prepare it a day ahead. Remember to make little slits in the sausages so they will lie flat.

HEITZ
CELLARS,
ST. HELENA
3-20-93

# 6. PASTA AND RICE

## LUISA'S FAVORITE CHICKEN AND PASTA CASSEROLE

There is nothing as easy and tasty as a big bubbling hot casserole of this all-time favorite of the opera singer, Luisa Tetrazzini. This is a perfect choice for a vineyard party. Serve with a green salad and plenty of hot buttered French bread, and of course, wine.

*1/2 lb. (8 oz.) spaghettini*
*3 cups diced and cooked boneless chicken breast (or other parts)*
*1/3 cup butter*
*3 T flour*
*2 cups half-and-half*
*salt and pepper to taste*
*1/4 tsp cayenne pepper (optional)*
*3 T sherry*
*1 medium green bell pepper, chopped*
*3/4 lb. mushrooms, thinly sliced*
*1 cup grated Parmesan cheese*
*minced parsley for garnish*

Cook the spaghettini as per package directions to "al dente." Do not let it become mushy. Drain and set aside.

In a saucepan, melt the butter. Blend in the flour and cook together a minute. Slowly add the half-and-half, stirring until the mixture is slightly thickened. This is a thin sauce. Add the salt, pepper, and cayenne if used. Stir in the green pepper, mushrooms, chicken and sherry. Blend well and set aside.

Lightly butter a 3-quart baking dish. Place the pasta on the bottom. Add the chicken sauce on top. Sprinkle with Parmesan. Cook, uncovered, in a 350° oven for 45 minutes. If you make Luisa's casserole ahead of time, just allow about 15-20 minutes extra time for baking. Garnish with a little minced parsley. This will serve 6 generously.

# SYLVIA SEBASTIANI'S SPAGHETTI SAUCE

Of the many recipes for spaghetti sauce I've tried, this one, from a wonderful California wine country lady, is the best. It has all the flavors and character of a true California Italian kitchen. It can be used with any pasta, but it is special with spaghetti.

> *1 lb. ground beef (optional)*
> *4 T olive oil*
> *4 T butter*
> *4 stalks celery, chopped*
> *4 onions, chopped*
> *4 cloves garlic, chopped fine*
> *1/4 tsp thyme*
> *1/4 tsp rosemary*
> *1/2 cup finely-chopped parsley*
> *1/2 cup dried Italian mushrooms,*
> *    soaked in 1 cup hot water and then chopped*
> *1 large (28-oz.) can solid pack tomatoes, mashed with liquid*
> *6 8-oz cans tomato sauce*
> *1-1/2 cups water*
> *1 cup Sebastiani Chablis, Green Hungarian,*
> *    Mountain Chablis, or Vin Rose*
> *1 tsp sugar*
> *salt and pepper to taste*

If using meat, brown it in olive oil and butter. Add celery and onions; sauté until brown, then add garlic. Salt and pepper to taste, then add spices, mushrooms with their liquid, tomatoes and tomato sauce. Rinse tomato sauce cans with water, and add to the sauce along with wine and sugar. Cook for 3 hours over low heat, stirring occasionally. If not using meat, start by browning onions and celery and proceed as above.

Instead of ground beef, a piece of pot roast can be used. Brown on all sides and proceed as above, letting meat simmer in sauce. After two hours, remove meat from sauce and keep warm. Slice and serve as a meat course for your dinner. If your family likes their sauce hot, add a small chili pepper, chopped very fine, while sauce is simmering. These peppers are very hot and go a long way, so use them with caution. This recipe yields a quantity of sauce greater than you would normally use at one time, so freeze the remainder in pint jars, filling 3/4 full. I always keep a supply of frozen sauce on hand -- it helps put together numerous meals in a short time.

KENWOOD VINEYARDS,
KENWOOD

## RICE WITH SOUR CREAM AND CHILES

There is always a great feeling of pride when you bring the perfect dish to a potluck party. This mixture is always a winner. It can easily be made the day ahead, and tastes good even after it cools. Variations can be made by tucking in a few bay shrimp, diced chicken breasts, or shredded roast pork.

*3 cups cooked rice (1 cup raw)*
*1 6-oz can Ortega diced chiles, or 4 fresh peeled chiles, diced*
*2 cups sour cream*
*salt and pepper to taste*
*1 tsp chili powder*
*1 tsp cumin seed (optional)*
*2 cups grated Jack or Cheddar cheese*
*1 tsp oil or butter*

Cook rice using your favorite method. Cool slightly. Add chili powder, cumin, salt and pepper. Mix in the sour cream and gently blend.

Rub the butter or oil into a 1-1/2 quart baking casserole. Place half the rice in the casserole. Divide the chiles in half and spoon half the chiles over the rice. Sprinkle half (1 cup) of the grated cheese over the chiles. Repeat with another layer of rice, chiles, and cheese. Bake in a 350° oven, uncovered, for 25 minutes. Garnish with fresh cilantro, a few diced tomatoes, or chopped black olives if desired. This will serve 6. If the dish has been refrigerated, increase the baking time by 15 minutes.

## WHITE WINE MACARONI AND CHEESE

A little white wine added to this traditional dish turns macaroni and cheese into a really special creation. Serve this as an accompaniment to a dinner entree, or as a main course in itself. For added interest, bits of chicken, ham or shrimp may be added. About 1 cup is perfect.

*2 cups elbow macaroni, small mostaccioli, or other small pasta*
*3 T butter*
*1/2 medium onion, chopped (1/4 cup)*
*3 T flour*
*1 cup milk or half-and-half*
*1/2 cup dry white wine*
*salt and pepper to taste*
*1/4 tsp cayenne pepper (optional)*
*2 cups grated sharp Cheddar cheese (about 1/2 lb.)*

Cook the pasta as per package directions, then drain. Do not over-cook. In a saucepan, melt the butter and add the onion. Cook until just limp. Add the flour and stir until well blended. Slowly add the milk and stir until the sauce is slightly thick. Add the wine (don't worry if it looks a little curdly) and then the cheese. Add the seasonings and stir until the cheese is melted.

Butter a 1-1/2 to 2 quart casserole. Add the drained pasta. Pour the sauce over the top and mix with the pasta. Bake at 350° for 25 minutes. A sprinkle of paprika may be added to the top for extra color. This will serve 4.

## SICILIAN EGGPLANT SAUCE FOR PASTA

Sicilian cooking is full of zesty and pungent flavors. This sauce, using eggplants grown and ripened in California valleys, is a favorite for pasta in the hot summer when eggplants are at their peak.

*1 whole eggplant, about 1-1/2 lbs.*
*5 T olive oil*
*2 garlic cloves, minced*
*1 tsp crushed, dried red pepper*
*1 T capers*
*1/4 cup lightly toasted pine nuts (optional)*
*1 15-oz can of tomato sauce*
*1 cup dry red wine*
*salt and pepper to taste*
*1 lb. spaghetti or pasta of your choice,*
*   cooked according to package directions*
*freshly-grated Parmesan cheese*

Peel and cut the eggplant into 3/4" cubes. Of course they will not come out a perfect square, but do the best you can. Place the cubes in a colander. With your hands, rub 1 tsp salt into the cubes. Leave in the colander for 30 minutes, then take some paper towels and blot the eggplant dry. This procedure removes the bitter juices from the eggplant.

In a large skillet, heat the oil. Add eggplant and garlic. Stir-fry until the eggplant is light brown and limp. Add tomato sauce, wine, dried red pepper, salt and pepper. Simmer over a low flame for 15 minutes, stirring now and then. Add capers and pine nuts (if used) and stir for a minute until blended. To serve, place some sauce on each portion of cooked pasta, topping with cheese and a little minced parsley. This will serve 4-5. The sauce may be made ahead and refrigerated.

LIPARITA HARVEST,
ANGWIN
2-27-92

# 7. SALADS

11·30·91
CALISTOGA

## STERLING VINEYARDS BABY ROMAINE SALAD WITH PARMESAN CURLS

Once, on a glider ride from Calistoga, I was able to see those lovely white Sterling buildings in the early morning light. They nestle on top of a bluff in a perfect composition. Sterling is one of the most interesting California wineries to visit. I was intrigued by the simplicity of this recipe from their culinary files. It is very attractive, with a crisp fresh taste.

If you are not able to find baby Romaine, simply use the inner leaves of a regular Romaine head. One large or two medium should be the right amount.

*4-5 heads of baby Romaine lettuce*
*1/2 cup Extra Virgin olive oil*
*2 T red wine vinegar*
*salt*
*freshly ground black pepper*
*Parmesan cheese curls, preferably aged Parmesan or Reggiano*

Wash and dry greens and chill. Toss with olive oil, salt and pepper to taste, then add vinegar and toss again. Sprinkle with cheese curls. (To make the curls, either shave the piece of Parmesan with a vegetable peeler, or use a mandolin-type slicer at a very thin setting.)

# SUNSHINE ORANGE SALAD

California tourist advertisements always seem to picture orange groves on a sunny day. This colorful salad reflects this spirit.

*3 oranges (Valencia or navel)*
*1 medium onion, red or white*
*1/2 cup sliced black olives, drained*
*freshly ground black pepper to taste*
*4 T olive oil*
*1/4 cup walnuts, lightly roasted and chopped*
*fresh parsley for garnish*

Peel the oranges and onion and slice into thin slices. In a shallow bowl, combine the oranges, onions and olives. Pour the olive oil over the salad and add pepper. Mix well to combine ingredients. Cover and place in a cool place for an hour to allow the flavors to mingle.

To serve, sprinkle the walnuts on top and garnish with a little fresh minced parsley. This will serve 4.

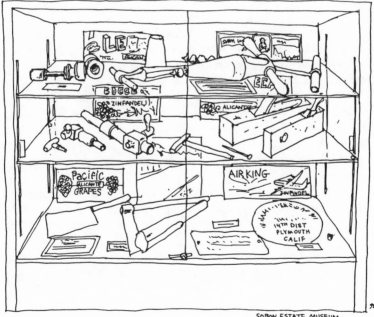

SOBON ESTATE MUSEUM,
PLYMOUTH

# HOLLYWOOD COBB SALAD

Up and down the state of California, Cobb salad is on restaurant menus and made in our kitchens. There are many versions, but there are some basic rules for preparing the salad. It must be made in layers, and only tossed just before serving. A large glass bowl is the perfect Cobb container. Assembling a Cobb salad is like painting a picture as you carefully layer all the colorful ingredients. This salad is a perfect dinner on a hot summer day, served with chilled wine.

*1/2 head iceberg lettuce*
*1/2 head chicory or endive lettuce*
*1/2 head romaine lettuce*
*1/2 bunch of watercress*
*2 ripe tomatoes, peeled and thinly sliced*
*2 T minced green onions or chives*
*6 slices of cooked crisp bacon, crumbled*
*3 hard-boiled eggs, peeled and chopped*
*1 ripe avocado, peeled and diced*
*2 chicken breasts, cooked, boned and diced*
*lemon juice*
*2 ozs. blue or Roquefort cheese, crumbled*

Wash the lettuce. Discard any bruised leaves. Wash the watercress, using only the top leaves. Wrap the lettuce and cress in a damp towel, place in a plastic bag and refrigerate. Dice the chicken breasts and moisten with fresh lemon juice.

To assemble, cut the greens very fine and place in your bowl (or on a platter). The chicken is the next layer, followed by the green onions and tomatoes. Sprinkle the bacon in a strip on the right hand side of the salad. The eggs go in a strip on the left. The avocado is placed around the sides, and finally add the blue cheese wherever you think it might look pretty.

You may use any French dressing, or make your own by combining 1/2 cup salad oil, 3 T red wine vinegar, 2 T lemon juice, 1 tsp salt, 1/4 tsp pepper, a pinch of mustard and a clove of minced garlic. This dressing may be made ahead.

To serve, bring the salad to the table. Pour dressing on the salad. Now mix all the pretty strips and things together. This will serve 4-5.

BOEGER WINERY
PLACERVILLE
4·23·92

## PROVENÇAL ONION SALAD

Reminders of the French influence are evident in wine country. Often this salad is part of a dinner party buffet. Onion salad is served slightly warm or at room temperature. Try it with your next barbecue for a delicious addition.

*6 medium onions, any variety*
   *(red or white or a nice combination)*
*4 T white wine*
*2 T olive oil*

Place the onions, unpeeled, in an oven-proof dish. Mix the wine and olive oil and pour over them. Bake uncovered at 350° for one hour. If the liquid dries out while baking, add a little more oil and wine. Set the onions aside after the baking and allow to cool enough to handle. Peel and slice the best you can -- baked onions are a little tricky to slice perfectly. Place the sliced onions in a pretty bowl and pour the following mixture over them:

*4 T olive oil*
*3 T red or white wine vinegar*
*1 tsp oregano, dried or fresh*
*salt and pepper to taste*

Mix together and blend with the onions. Garnish with some snipped fresh parsley. This will serve 4

# WINTER PEAR AND ENDIVE SALAD

This salad is lovely, with the smooth texture of pears and the slight crunch of endive. Watercress adds a nip that is very refreshing. If fresh pomegranates are in season, sprinkle some seeds over the top of the salad. This is especially colorful during the holiday season.

*4 ripe pears*
*1 lb. Belgian endive*
*1 bunch fresh watercress*
*2-3 T pomegranate seeds (optional)*
*1/4 cup white wine vinegar*
*1/2 cup peanut or other salad oil*
*salt and pepper to taste*

Peel and core the pears and cut into long wedges, about 1/3" wide. Wash and stem endive and cut across in 3/4" slices. Remove stems from watercress, wash and dry the leaves.

Combine vinegar and oil with salt and pepper in a bowl. Mix with a fork. Add the other ingredients and toss lightly. This will serve 4 generously. If you wish to make a salad main dish, simply add some slivered chicken breasts or cooked little bay shrimp.

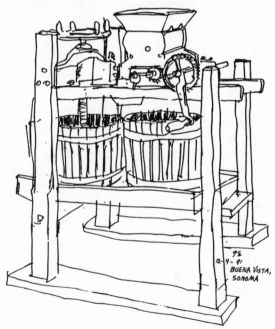

BUENA VISTA,
SONOMA

12-4-91
SEBASTIANI,
SONOMA

## SYLVIA SEBASTIANI'S BEAN AND TUNA SALAD

This favorite salad from a respected Sonoma Valley classic cook is wonderful as a side dish with buffets or a summer lunch. It takes only a few minutes to assemble.

*1 15-oz. can kidney beans*
*1/2 cup red onion, chopped*
*1 6-1/2 oz. can tuna*
*4 T oil*
*2 T finely chopped parsley*
*1 clove garlic, minced*
*1 T wine vinegar*
*salt and pepper to taste*

Drain and wash beans in a colander. Mix all ingredients in a bowl, adding salt and pepper to taste. Chill and serve. This serves 4-6, and is great for barbeques during the summer months.

10-18-91
SONOMA PLAZA

MADRONA MANOR
HEALDSBURG  3·19·92

# 8. VEGETABLES

9E
10-18-91
BERINGER HOUSE,
ST. HELENA

## RHINELAND RED CABBAGE

The Beringer brothers came to Napa Valley from Mainz on the Rhine. The famous Rhine house is a replica of a Rhenish family castle.

It serves as a hospitality center for visitors. The winery, founded in 1876, is the oldest in the valley.

This succulent red cabbage, flavored with red wine, is one of the many popular recipes from Germany that have found their way into wine country cuisine.

*2 T butter or bacon drippings*
*1 apple, peeled and sliced*
*1 onion, peeled and sliced*
*1 T sugar*
*1 medium head of red cabbage, sliced thin*
*1 cup of red wine*
*1 cup liquid (water or broth)*
*salt and pepper to taste*

Melt the butter or drippings in a heavy saucepan. Add apple, onion and sugar. Fry just until limp, about 5 minutes. Add cabbage, red wine, liquid, salt and pepper. Stir together to blend ingredients.

Cover and bake in a 325° oven for one hour, or simmer over a low flame on top of the stove. Check the liquid now and then, adding more wine if necessary. This will serve 4-5.

# DELICATO VINEYARDS BROCCOLI IN WHITE WINE

This recipe is by Arlene Mueller, co-author of the Delicato cookbook "Wine, Food and the Good Life." It is a uniquely delicious way of preparing broccoli. Delicato Vineyards, in Manteca, is a half-century-old family winery.

*1 large bunch broccoli*
*1/2 cup California dry white wine*
*3 T olive oil*
*2 garlic cloves, slivered*
*2 T lemon juice*
*2 T minced parsley*

Wash broccoli, removing leaves, trimming flowerettes, and cutting stems into 1/2" pieces. Steam stem pieces until almost tender (about 15 minutes). Add flowerettes to stems and steam until both are tender but not mushy (about 5 minutes).

In a separate saucepan, simmer the wine, oil, garlic, lemon juice and parsley for 10 minutes. Place the broccoli in a heated serving bowl, pour the hot sauce over it, and toss lightly. This will make 4 to 6 portions.

The garlic may be increased in this recipe, if you like. The sauce is also good on other vegetables, including boiled potatoes.

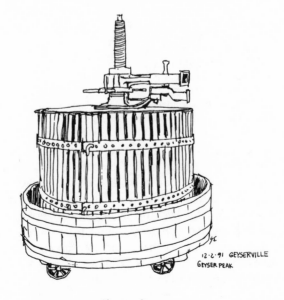

12-2-91 GEYSERVILLE
GEYSER PEAK

LUTHER BURBANK'S HOUSE, SANTA ROSA

2·27·92

## BURBANK WINE SCALLOPED POTATOES

Luther Burbank came to Santa Rosa in 1873 to continue his horticultural career. He financed his trip to California by selling his rights to his "Burbank Potato." Burbank was a real plant wizard, full of energy. He would sometimes have 3000 plant experiments going at once.

Potatoes are greatly enhanced by white wine in this tasty version of scalloped potatoes. If you have leftovers, they are delicious served cold with a sandwich.

*3-4 medium potatoes*
*1/2 lb. thinly sliced Swiss cheese*
*2 peeled and sliced onions*
*2 T Dijon-style mustard*
*salt and pepper to taste*
*1 cup dry white wine*
*1/4 cup Parmesan cheese*
*butter for dish and topping, about 3 T*

Peel the potatoes and cut, crossways, into slices about 1/3" thick. Divide in thirds. Butter a large pie pan (9-1/2" diameter, or 8x8" square pan). Lay one third of the potatoes in the dish. Sprinkle with salt and pepper and spread lightly with half of the mustard. Add half of the cheese slices, followed by slices of one onion. Repeat another layer of each, and top with the remaining potato slices. Pour wine over dish. Top with Parmesan cheese and dot with butter. Cover with foil and bake at 350° for 30 minutes. Remove cover and bake an additional 20 minutes. This will serve 4 generously.

## CALIFORNIA CARROTS

Fresh California carrots are sweet and tender. Although everyone knows that carrots are good for you and brimming with vitamins, sometimes they may be overlooked as a vegetable choice. This wine-flavored recipe is delicious and makes a healthy addition to any meal.

*1 lb fresh carrots*
*2 T butter*
*1 clove garlic, minced*
*1 medium onion, finely chopped*
*salt and pepper to taste*
*1 cup dry white wine*
*1 tsp grated orange peel*
*1 T honey*
*toasted chopped almonds (optional)*

Grate the carrots and place in a bowl. Melt butter in sauce pan. Add the garlic and onion, and cook just until soft. Add carrots, salt, pepper and white wine. Cook, uncovered, for 10 minutes. Add the honey and orange peel, cover, and cook a few more minutes. Serve hot, sprinkled with a few toasted almonds if desired. This will serve 4-5. It may also be served cool.

*7L
9-14-91
LAPARITA VINEYARD,
ANGWIN*

## DELICATO'S MARINATED ONIONS

This is a cool, refreshing relish to serve with ham, and is also excellent with ham and rye sandwiches. This recipe, another from Delicato cookbook author Arlene Mueller, makes a refreshing tasty addition to any party table.

*4 cups thinly sliced Bermuda onions*
*1 tsp salt*
*1/8 tsp white pepper*
*2 cups California dry white wine*
*Parsley sprigs for garnish*

Place onions, salt and pepper in wine. Chill for several hours or overnight. Garnish with parsley sprigs. This will make 4 cups.

For a variation with a brighter, rosier look, substitute red onions and Delicato Rosé or Cabernet, and use plenty of grated black pepper.

LILLIE LANGTRY HOUSE
GUENOC VINEYARDS & WINERY,
NAPA

# 9. DESSERTS

## LAKE COUNTRY POACHED PEARS

On the quiet roads in the Northern California lake country you can still see some pear orchards, although vineyards have replaced many of these fruit growing areas. It was a natural to combine pears and wine in a refreshing popular dessert.

> *4 ripe pears*
> *1 lemon, juice and grated rind*
> *3 cups dry red wine*
> *1 cup sugar*
> *1 tsp cinnamon*

The pears need to be just ripe. If they are too soft, they will not hold up in this recipe. Peel the pears, leaving the stem on. In a saucepan place the lemon juice, rind, wine, sugar and cinnamon. Add the pears. Bring the mixture to a simmer and give a stir. Cover and cook for about 10 minutes. The pears should be just barely tender. Watch carefully that you don't overcook. If the liquid does not completely cover the pears while cooking, just roll them around so that all sides are coated. Cool in the syrup. This will serve 4, and may be served at room temperature or chilled.

# GUENOC BROWNIES FROM KAREN MELANDER-MAGOON

Karen is the most dynamic and fun lady I have met while working on this book.  As manager of marketing and public relations at Guenoc, her enthusiasm is unbounded.  It is easy to be passionate about Guenoc, as the 300 acres of vineyards are in one of the most beautiful valleys in California.  This was the home of the famous Victorian actress and beauty Lillie Langry, who hoped to produce on this ranch the greatest claret in the county.  Her home has been preserved and is used for special events at Guenoc.  Today their wines have won the highest awards in the world.  Karen has great style in matching food with wine.  Her delicious brownies are served with Guenoc Petite Sirah.

*3 ozs. unsweetened chocolate*
*6 T butter*
*1-1/2 cups sugar*
*3 eggs*
*1/4 tsp salt*
*3/4 cup flour*
*1 cup chopped walnuts*
*1-1/2 tsp vanilla*

Preheat oven to 350°.  Butter an 8" or 9" square cake pan (you may find buttering only the bottom works best).  Melt the chocolate and butter together in a double boiler or in a pan over simmering water, stirring until smooth.  Remove from heat and stir in the sugar, eggs, salt, flour, walnuts and vanilla.  Combine well.

Spread the mixture in the pan.  Bake for about 35-40 minutes until dry on top and almost firm to the touch.  Set the pan on a rack to cool for about 15 minutes, then cut the brownies into 2-1/4" squares.  Serve warm with Guenoc Petite Sirah.

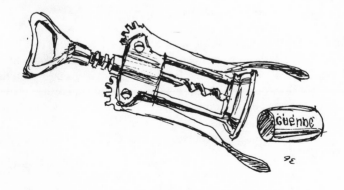

## GUENOC BROWNIES FROM JACKIE

The Guenoc winery tasting room is housed in a rambling, state-of-the-art, 54,000-square-foot winery. The tastings are generous and everyone is greeted like an old friend. This is where I first heard about the Guenoc brownie recipes. This one, from Jackie Henkelman, their hospitality coordinator, is unusual for its use of macadamia nuts, which add a magical crunch to these terrific brownies.

*10 ounces sweet chocolate*
*3 4-oz cubes of sweet butter*
*4 cups sugar*
*1 T vanilla*
*2 cups unbleached flour*
*6 eggs, beaten*
*1 oz. brandy*
*2 cups chopped macadamia nuts*

Melt the chocolate and butter in a double boiler. Remove to a bowl, cool slightly, add beaten eggs and mix well. Next add sugar, vanilla and brandy. Mix well. Add the flour, a half-cup at a time. Add the nuts. Pour into a buttered 11x18" baking dish. This size pan is known as a jelly roll pan. If you do not have one, you can divide the dough between two 8" square pans. Bake at 350° for 55 minutes. Do not overcook. Cool on rack and cut into squares. Serve with Guenoc Winery Petite Sirah.

## ROBERT LOUIS STEVENSON OATMEAL COOKIES

One of the most memorable tales written about the Napa Valley is Stevenson's "Silverado Squatters." The story is about the experiences of Stevenson and his wife Fanny, living in a rustic miner's cabin high above Calistoga, near the famed Silverado mine.

Stevenson's domestic duties for the morning consisted of starting the fire in the stove for oatmeal porridge and coffee. The Scots have a passion for oatmeal. As a tribute to this beloved author, oatmeal cookies are a favorite for wine country picnics. This is an "icebox" cookie -- the dough is made ahead, chilled, sliced, and baked as the cookies are needed.

*1 cup shortening (can be half butter)*
*1 cup brown sugar*
*1 cup white sugar*
*2 eggs, beaten*
*1 tsp vanilla*
*1-1/2 cups flour*
*1 tsp salt*
*1 tsp baking soda*
*3 cups uncooked oatmeal (do not use instant)*
*1/2 cup chopped walnuts (optional)*

Cream the shortening and sugar together until light and fluffy. Add eggs and vanilla. Blend into a creamy mixture. Sift the dry ingredients and add to the mixture in the bowl. Mix well. Stir in the oats and nuts.

When well mixed, shape into rolls of desired diameter. Wrap in waxed paper and chill at least four hours. The dough will keep up to a week in the refrigerator, or longer in the freezer. When you're ready to bake the cookies, slice the dough into 1/4" slices with a sharp knife. Bake on an ungreased cookie sheet for 10 minutes at 350°. Remove from sheet and cool on a rack. This will make 4-5 dozen cookies.

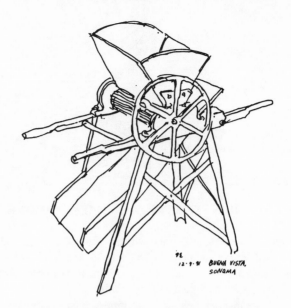

12·7·91  BUENA VISTA,
SONOMA

## JENNY'S WHITE WINE WEDDING CAKE

Wineries are a popular place for weddings. Often the couple will take their vows under a grape leaf canopy. This is a lovely and romantic moment. A wedding cake will be waiting for the couple to proceed with the traditional cake-cutting ceremony. My daughter, Jeanne, and special friends made this cake for our dear family friend Jenny. This cake is very easy to make, and the white wine adds a tantalizing flavor and moistness.

*2 cups sugar*
*4 eggs*
*1 cup vegetable oil*
*1 cup dry white wine*
*2-1/2 cups cake flour (regular can be substituted)*
*1/2 tsp salt*
*2-1/2 tsp baking powder*
*1 tsp vanilla*

In a mixing bowl, beat the eggs and sugar together for 30 seconds. Sift the dry ingredients. Add the oil, wine, vanilla and dry ingredients together to the egg mixture. Mix for one minute, making sure everything is blended. Grease and flour two 9" round cake pans (or 9x9" square ones) and pour in the batter. Bake at 350° for 30 minutes. Remove from cake pans and cool on racks. Frost as desired. For weddings, repeat this recipe as many times as needed.

MADRONA VINEYARDS,
PLACERVILLE

# 10. VISITING WINERIES

# VISITING WINERIES

A California winery might be in a tiny shed or in a huge modern building. The one thing they have in common is a warmth and eagerness to share their wine creations with you. Each winery takes great pride in its product, and every single wine has its own character. No two are ever the same. You do not need to be a wine expert to enjoy winery visits; wines are always explained by the friendly host or hostess. Remember, wine is not complicated; after all, it is basically fermented grape juice.

It is not possible to list here all of the thousands of wineries in our state. The wineries included here are just some of the most historic and fun. Opening hours are not listed, as they vary from season to season, so it is best to check by phone or with local information sources.

## BERINGER VINEYARDS
2000 Main St., St. Helena      (707)963-7115

You can't miss the landmark Rhine house modeled after the Beringer house in Germany. Visiting Beringer, with their outstanding tour guides, is one of the most interesting Napa valley experiences. Everyone enjoys seeing the original aging tunnels dug by Chinese workers. Beringer is known for their Chardonnay and Cabernet.

## BOEGER,
1709 Carson Rd., Placerville   (916) 622-8094

The tasting room at Boeger is listed in the National Register of Historic Places as one of America's oldest wineries. The walls date back to 1870 and are two feet thick. The family lived upstairs, and would stomp the grapes which flowed down chutes (still present) to ferment in the barrels on the ground floor. In this rustic winery there are flowers, pear and ancient fig trees, with picnic tables scattered here and there.

## BUENA VISTA
18000 Old Winery Rd., Sonoma    (707) 938-1266

This winery was founded in 1857 by the colorful Hungarian Agoston Haraszhy. He was the father of California viticulture, bringing 100,000 wine cuttings from Europe to California. Tasting is in the original press room, which has a balcony with very good art exhibits. Snacks are available for the terraced picnic area. The front patio is shaded by giant eucalyptus trees, which add to this very old winery. Fumé Blanc and Zinfandel rate high with the tasters.

## CALLAWAY VINEYARD AND WINERY
32720 Rancho California Rd., Temecula    (714) 676-4001
Callaway is Southern California's largest premium winery. It is the oldest of the Temecula wineries, located on 720 acres of rolling vineyards. The tasting room is on a hill with lovely views of the surrounding vineyards. There is an attractive picnic area under a vine-covered arbor. The facility offers picnic supplies and gifts.

## CLINE CELLARS
24737 Arnold Dr., Sonoma    (707) 935-4310
Cline Cellars is located on the original site of the Mission San Francisco de Solano. There are natural springs which the Cline family is restoring to the original carp ponds. The tasting room is in an 1850 farm house. The specialty is California Rhone-style wines. Call for information on their winemaker lunches and other events.

## CHATEAU ST. JEAN
8555 Sonoma Hwy, Kenwood    (707)833-4134
One of the most attractive views of the valley is from the medieval tower in the winery. There is a self-guided tour with vistas of the winemaking process. Chardonnay and Sauvignon Blanc are two of the favorite wines here.

## DELICATO
12001 S. Highway 99, Manteca    (209) 239-1215
An informative guided tour of this San Joaquin Valley winery will show you all the fermentors, redwood tanks, and the bottling line. There is an interesting gift store. A wide range of wines include dessert and sparkling wines at reasonable prices.

## DOMAINE MICHEL
4155 Wine Creek Rd., Healdsburg (707) 433-7427
Jean-Jacques Michel is from Geneva, and visited Sonoma in the 1970s. He had a dream of creating a winery in this area and was able to purchase land by Wine Creek Road. The name of this road originated during Prohibition times, when wine was

dumped into the creek by illegal vintners. There is an early Mission-style tasting room on this enjoyable 100-acre estate. You do need reservations to tour this winery. Chardonnay and Cabernet are hits.

## FETZER
13500 S. Highway 101, Hopland    (707) 744-1747
The tasting and gift store are housed in the old Hopland high school, a large, impressive and fun center. Fetzer wines are reasonably priced and of excellent quality.

## FIRESTONE
5017 Zaca Station Rd., Los Olivos    (805) 688-3940
Brooks Firestone has in the last 18 years achieved a worldwide reputation with his wines from the Santa Ynez Valley. This is a very well-run vineyard. The tour is one of the best in the state and all the personnel very helpful. Their Rosé and Cabernet are very popular, as are their various Riesling varieties.

## GEYSER PEAK
22281 Chianti Rd., Geyserville    (707) 433-6585
The tasting room is housed in an ivy-covered stone building which is part of a 100-year-old structure. There are hiking trails and picnic areas. The wines are fairly priced, clean and favorable. You can buy wine vinegar in the tasting room.

## GLEN ELLEN WINERY
1883 London Ranch Rd., Glen Ellen  (707) 935-3047
Nestled in a pretty valley with white clapboard buildings, this is the home of the Benziger family, which includes seven children and their families. Visitors may picnic in the redwood grove. Along with the popular Glen Ellen wines, they also produce M.G. Vallejo and their upscale Benziger series.

## GRGICH HILLS CELLAR
1829 St. Helena Hwy, Rutherford    (707) 963-2784
One of the most popular winemakers in California, Mike Grgich is originally from Yugoslavia and arrived in Napa Valley in 1958. He worked with famed winemaker Andre Tchelistcheff at Beaulieu Vineyards, and then with Robert Mondavi. On July 4, 1977, he was able to open his own winery with Austin Hills. Best known for its Chardonnay, the Zinfandel and Cabernet are

also outstanding.

## GUENOC WINERY
21000 Butts Canyon Rd., Middletown   (707) 987-9127

Orville Magoon, Guenoc winegrower, is a Renaissance man. In addition to his fame as a coastal civil engineer, he and his wife Karen Melander-Magoon have won awards for the best wines in the world. From the winery and tasting room you can overlook the valley panorama as you picnic. There are 300 acres of vineyard. Guenoc was the home of the famed beauty and actress Lilly Langtry, whose home is open for special occasions. Petite Sirah, Merlot and Chardonnay are some of the award-winning favorites.

## HESS COLLECTION
4411 Redwood Rd., Napa       (707) 255-1144

On the slopes of Mr. Veeder on the site of the 1903 Gier Winery, Donald Hess (heir to a Swiss brewing and natural water company) and his American wife decided to create a vineyard in this unique area, 2000 feet above the valley floor. The grapes are all hand-picked and the wines full and rich. Cabernet Sauvignon and Chardonnay are the stars. One entire level of the handsome stone building is devoted to the Hess collection of contemporary art, which includes works by Stella, Motherwell and others.

## HEITZ WINE CELLARS
436 S. St. Helena Hwy., St. Helena     (707) 963-3452

Joe and Alice Heitz are treasures of the California vintners' world. They had a dream of owning their own vineyard to produce the best wines possible. Heitz cellars opened in 1961 and since then, with the help of their three children, they have won awards world wide. The tasting room is simple but the sampling generous. The actual winery is located on their ranch in an 1800s stone cellar. All the wines, especially the Zinfandel and Grignolino, are winners. This is one of the few wineries to make Angelica, a dessert wine from California's past.

## HOP KILN WINERY
6050 Westside Rd., Healdsburg     (707) 433-6491

Hop Kiln is a registered historical landmark, and well it should be. It is a genuine hop kiln. Photographs on the wall show how the hops processing worked. There is usually an art exhibit on the old wooden walls. Their red wines are hearty and they make a nice sparkling wine. The lovely picnic area, under 100-year-old fig trees, overlooks a pond with ducks and migrating birds.

## KENDALL-JACKSON
640 Matthews Rd., Lakeport    (707) 263-5299
The tasting room is in a cheery adobe building. The wines are all well-made and the Sauvignon Blanc is especially nice. The picnic area, amidst trees, is pleasant.

## KENWOOD VINEYARDS
9592 Sonoma Hwy., Kenwood    (707) 833-5891
Kenwood converted a 1906 winery into a modern wood-faced ranch-style building. The tasting room is airy and stylish, offering attractive gift items. Pinot Noir and Chenin Blanc are among the favorite wines here. There is a picnic area within the neatly landscaped yard.

## MADRONA VINEYARDS
High Hill Rd., Camino    (916) 644-5948
The road to Madrona wanders past an Apple Pie House and a fudge factory. This area is especially busy during the fall apple season, and so is the winery. Located by Madrona trees (this is where the name originated), this is the highest (3000 feet) winery in the state. The grapes on these 35 scenic acres of vineyards are hand picked. The carefully-made wines are outstanding, especially the Zinfandel and Cabernet Franc. Picnic tables are scattered around in this rustic country setting.

## MIRASSOU VINEYARDS
3000 Aborn Rd., San Jose    (408) 274-4000
The Mirassou family has been growing grapes in Santa Clara Valley since 1854. Their wines are well-respected. The grounds are tree-shaded and the buildings nicely weathered. Tastings are generous and there is a gift store. The Mirassou wines are especially popular for holiday gifts.

## ROBERT MONDAVI WINERY
7801 St. Helena Hwy., Oakville    (707) 963-9611
Mondavi is the third largest producer of wines in Napa Valley. The mission-style winery is a landmark and offers excellent

tours, art exhibits, concerts, food seminars, wine tasting dinners, and a Great Chefs program. Among the distinguished wines are their Pinot Noir and Fumé Blanc. The gift store is popular.

## MONTEVINO WINERY

20680 Shenandoah School Rd., Plymouth    (209) 245-6942

Amador County has a heritage of excellent red wines due to the unique soil and climate. Montevino is known for Italian-style red wines. You can taste them all in this spacious tasting room. There is room for 200 picnics on their covered patios. The winemaker is excited about their Barbera 1987 reserve.

## MOUNT PALOMAR WINERY

33820 Rancho California Rd., Temecula    (714) 676-5047

The pleasant tasting room has a rustic barn-like quality. On the wood walls hang the many prize ribbons awarded to the winery. Their Reislings are big winners and the "table" variety will add a cheerful touch to your picnic. There is an excellent assortment of picnic food supplies and a deli. Tables are scattered around the grounds.

## PARDUCCI WINE CELLARS

501 Parducci Rd., Ukiah    (707) 462-9463

This family winery, in a pleasant sort of Mission-style building, dates back to 1931. The hour-long tour is informative. In addition to wine-related gifts, there is also a crystal and china store. Prices are moderate for these well-respected wines, and there are special prices for cases. The white wine selections are especially popular.

## RIDGE

17100 Montebello Rd., Cupertino    (408) 867-3233

The largest and most respected of the Santa Cruz mountain wineries is set on a mountain ridge with spectacular views. Their Zinfandel and Cabernet Sauvignon have won awards world wide. Ridge fans are sort of like a red wine cult, and other wine makers adore Ridge. Bring a picnic to enjoy the mood and setting. Remember, Ridge is only open on weekends for tasting.

## SAN ANTONIO WINERY/MADDALENA VINEYARDS

737 Lamar St., Los Angeles    (213) 223-1401

San Antonio is only a few miles away from the first vineyard in Los Angeles. The grape vines planted by Louis Vignes in 1830 have vanished, and downtown Los Angeles stands where they grew. San Antonio carries on the Los Angeles tradition. The comfortable tasting room has an adjoining room for gifts and another for parties catered by the family restaurant, Maddalena's. The Riboli family, owners of the winery, produce good table wines and also a selection of premium wines. There is a shaded picnic area for 100, popular with downtown employees.

## V. SATTUI WINERY

1111 White Lane (Hwy 29), St. Helena   (707) 963-7774

Where is the best spot in Napa Valley to purchase food for picnics? Without a doubt, it is Sattui. Salami and an array of beautiful meats are sliced fresh for you. Sandwiches will be prepared with your favorite combinations. Did you need plates, forks, napkins? They are all here at reasonable prices. The wine-related gift store is full of great items, and there are picnic tables outside the winery. V. Sattui wine can only be purchased here at the winery. The wines have won many medals and any of them will go well with your picnic lunch.

## SEBASTIANI VINEYARDS

389 Fourth St., Sonoma     (707) 938-5532

The Sebastiani tour is one of the most interesting in Sonoma. You will view the red wine fermentors and the wonderfully carved barrels created by Earle Brown, walk along an elevated walkway to view the crushers (this is fun in harvest season), and then enjoy tasting the excellent wines. Barbera, Zinfandel and Merlot are among the favorites.

## SOBON ESTATE

14430 Shenandoah Rd., Plymouth   (209) 245-6555

Sobon is located in one of the oldest vineyards, dating to 1856. It was in former days the D'Agostini winery. The museum housed in the old winery is one of the most extensive and interesting in the state. There is a gift shop and room for picnics. Sobon is a perfect place for children to learn something about wine history.

## STERLING VINEYARDS

1111 Dunaweal Lane, Calistoga     (707) 942-5151

Sterling offers one of the most unique wine tours in California. You ride on the sky tram to reach the gleaming white Moorish-style winery on top of the hill. The tour is self-guiding and very informative. The gift store has a touch of class. There are tables and chairs for a relaxing rest while enjoying the views. Sterling wines are some of the valley's best; enjoy the Chardonnay and Sauvignon Blanc.

## SUNRISE WINERY

13100 Montebello Rd., Cupertino     (408) 741-1310

These old stone and wood buildings are from the Picchetti ranch. Wine was made here over a hundred years ago. There is a gift store, picnic grounds and sometimes musical groups on weekends. Zinfandel and Pinot Blanc are among the best choices.

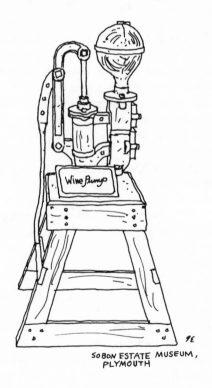

SOBON ESTATE MUSEUM,
PLYMOUTH

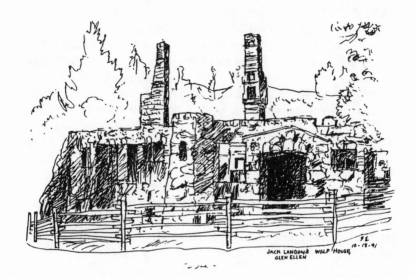

JACK LONDON & WOLF HOUSE
GLEN ELLEN
10-18-91

## CALIFORNIA WINE COUNTRY SIGHTS

Diverse sights relating to wine country history can be found up and down the state. They might be an old family winery, historic building, an author's home, or perhaps the favorite sight of all, which is miles of beautiful vineyards stretching from north to south in California.

### BALE GRIST MILL HISTORIC PARK
Highway 29, 3 miles N of St. Helena     (707)963-2236
A reminder of days when the land now occupied by vine-yards was used for wheat. This mill was used for over 35 years to grind flour. Photographers find this scenic mill a favorite shot.

### LUTHER BURBANK HOME AND GARDENS
corner Santa Rosa and Sonoma Ave., Santa Rosa
(707) 524-5445
Luther Burbank was America's most famous horticulturalist, and helped the wine industry with his grape stock research. You may visit his home and greenhouse. Exhibits relating to his life and work are housed in the carriage house. Open hours vary with the seasons, so be sure to call ahead.

## CALISTOGA DEPOT AND SHOPS

1458 Lincoln Ave., Calistoga

Built in 1868 for Sam Brannan's train, which brought people from San Francisco to Calistoga. Famed as one of the oldest depots in the state, it has been converted into shops and a helpful chamber of commerce.

## CALISTOGA MUD BATHS

The natural hot springs of Calistoga were known by early Indians for their healing powers. Today visitors come from all over to indulge in mud baths. Volcanic ash, clay and peat moss are heated to 104 degrees for this unique experience. Choose your favorite bath establishment!

## FETZER VALLEY OAKS FOOD AND WINE CENTER,

Hopland   (707) 744-1250

There are over four acres of bio-intensive organic gardening in this lovely spot. Culinary research and a cooking school with John Ash add to the center. Call ahead for current hours and school information.

## HURD BEESWAX

3020 St. Helena Highway N, St. Helena

If candles are your interest, this store and candle factory has every imaginable size and shape to offer. You can watch the fascinating process of candle making.

## HOT AIR BALLOON RIDES

This is a popular pastime and there are many companies offering this experience. Check the advertisements or ask for recommendations from your hotel.

## JIMTOWN STORE

6706 State Highway 128, Healdsburg   (707) 433-1212

Jimtown Store, in Alexander Valley, has been in business since 1893. There is freshly brewed coffee, excellent espresso, sandwiches, sweets, freshly baked goods, memorabilia and locally made gift items.

## JACK LONDON BOOK STORE
14300 Arnold Dr., Glen Ellen   (707) 433-1212

Russ and Winnie Kingman offer a wealth of knowledge on the local history scene. The specialty of this wonderful book store is Jack London. There is a great selection of London's books and many books relating to California.

## JACK LONDON STATE HISTORICAL PARK
London Ranch Road, Glen Ellen   (707) 938-5216

Within this magnificent 800 acres you can visit the Jack London Museum housed in Charmain London's "House of the Happy Walls," as well as the remains of Wolf House, Jack London's grave, and other historic sites. There is a lovely picnic area on this beautiful ranch.

## MARSHALL GOLD DISCOVERY STATE HISTORIC PARK
Colma   (916) 622-3470

On the way to the Sierra Foothill wineries, this is a lovely place to stop and visit the place where gold was discovered in California. There are plenty of picnic tables.

## NAPA VALLEY WINE TRAIN
1275 McKinstrey at Soscol Ave., Napa (707) 253-2111

What a pleasure it is to ride this train slowly along the vineyards, while enjoying lunch or dinner in the dining car. The service is great. Meals are prix fixe  and very well done. After the main course you move to the parlor car for coffee and dessert. There is also wine tasting for a small fee. Although there is some controversy about the train, it is very popular and provides a view of the landscape different from any other. One word of caution: figure out your way to the Napa depot ahead of time, as it can be difficult to find.

## NAPA VALLEY WINE LIBRARY COLLECTION
St. Helena Public Library, St. Helena   (707) 963-3535

This association has amassed a great collection of books relating to wine, all in one attractive room in the library. You can sit and read all about the history of California vineyards. There is a complete collection of M.F.K. Fisher books. The association presents seminars and classes about wine throughout the year.

## SHARPSTEEN MUSEUM AND SAM BRANNAN COTTAGE
1311 Washington St., Calistoga   (707) 942-5911
Open daily at noon.
Step back into the early days of Calistoga with historic dioramas and artifacts from the era. This museum was the project of Ben Sharpsteen and his wife, Bernice. Ben retired to Calistoga after a career with Disney Studios, and wanted to make this contribution to Calistoga's history. There is a book and gift store, and one of the original Brannan cottages.

## SILVERADO ROBERT LOUIS STEVENSON MUSEUM
1490 Library Lane, St. Helena   (707) 963-3757
Open 12-4 except Monday
If you are a Stevenson fan, this is the place to visit. It is the world's most outstanding collection of Stevenson memorabilia, and a calm and quiet museum worth spending time in.

CALISTOGA INN
3-19-92

## PLACES TO SPEND THE NIGHT

There is a varied assortment of lodgings in California Wine country, including historic houses, new and old motels, inns and a mixture of small bed-and-breakfasts. The atmosphere is warm and friendly, and in keeping with the vineyard tradition, complimentary wine is usually offered.

### BEST WESTERN DRY CREEK INN
198 Dry Creek Rd., Healdsburg    (800) 222-5784
One of the best values in this area. There are 104 rooms, and a complimentary bottle of wine and Continental breakfast are provided in the lobby. The location is one mile from the Russian River and convenient to touring.

### CALISTOGA INN
1250 Lincoln Ave., Calistoga    (707) 942-4101
This historic building, built at the turn of the century, offers 18 rooms (some without bathrooms). This inn is atmospheric with an excellent dining room and on-site brewery. A complimentary glass of wine or beer and Continental breakfast are included in their most reasonable prices.

### EL BONITA MOTEL
195 Main St., St. Helena    (707) 963-3216
El Bonita is cosy and offers a relaxing change from larger establishments. The friendly office staff pours fresh coffee and provides all kinds of information on wine touring and restaurants. The prices are moderate.

## GRAPE LEAF INN

539 Johnson St., Healdsburg    (707) 433-8140

The Grape Leaf is a refurbished 1900 Queen Anne Victorian home. There are seven rooms and a lovely shaded yard. The breakfast included in the price is outstanding.

## HARVEST INN,

1 Main St., St. Helena    (800) 950-8466

Tudor-style cottages are placed amid lovely gardens. The rooms are furnished with antiques. There is a swimming pool and spa. A most convenient and classy location.

SUTTER CREEK INN,
SUTTER CREEK

## HEALDSBURG INN ON THE PLAZA

110 Matheson St., Healdsburg    (707) 433-6991

Originally a 1900 Wells Fargo building, this inn offers refreshments in the solarium and a country breakfast. It is fun to stay in this location overlooking the lovely Healdsburg Square.

## JACK LONDON LODGE

13740 Arnold Dr., Glen Ellen    (707) 938-8510

This quiet motel-lodge at the entrance to Jack London State Park is a sentimental favorite of mine. It was the place we stayed on our first visit to the wine country and M.F.K. Fisher. The lodge is peaceful, with a creek and pool.

MADONNA INN

100 Madonna Rd., San Luis Obispo    (800) 543-9666

Of course it is gaudy, but it is fun and, with 109 rooms, a most convenient place to rest while visiting the central coast vineyards.


MADRONA MANOR

1001 Westside Rd., Healdsburg    (800) 258-4003

The Manor is an 1881 Victorian three-story mansion with 18 rooms and three suites.  Wooded acres and lovely gardens surround the mansion.  The dining room is justly famed.  Surely this is the perfect place for very special occasions.


MOUNT VIEW HOTEL

1457 Lincoln Ave., Calistoga    (707) 942-6877

Located on the main street of Calistoga, this hotel, built in 1912, has been remodeled in a sort of Art Deco style.  The hotel is an historic landmark and offers a complimentary European breakfast as well as excellent dining in Valeriano's Restaurant, located in the hotel.


NANCES HOT SPRINGS

1614 Lincoln Ave., Calistoga    (707) 942-6211

This landmark since 1923, located next to the glider field, offers moderate prices, mud and mineral baths.  Owned by the friendly Hughes family, this is a unique spot to stay.

PINK MANSION,
CALISTOGA
3-20-92

## THE PINK MANSION
1415 Foothill Blvd., Calistoga    (707) 942-0558

On top of the hill approaching Calistoga is this restored 1875 pink Victorian home. There are five beautiful furnished rooms, all with Calistoga views and moods. A top-of-the-line breakfast is served each morning, and there is an afternoon wine tasting. Visitors return each year, as spending the night in this pink palace is a treat.

## SUTTER CREEK INN
75 Main St., Sutter Creek       (209) 267-5606

This Greek Revival-style house is a charming place to relax while visiting the Sierra Foothills winery and gold country sights. The gardens are lovely, and there is a library with a fireplace and comfy couches. A full breakfast is included in the room price.

## TEMECULA CREEK INN
44501 Rainbow Canyon Rd., Temecula Valley    (714) 676-5631

You can play golf and visit the area wineries while staying in this attractive inn overlooking the valley.

## THATCHER INN,
Highway 101, Hopland    (707) 744-1890

The Thatcher is a Victorian country inn built in 1890, with twenty beautifully decorated guest rooms. The dining room offers a full country breakfast included in your room price. Nearby sights include the famed Hopland brewery and Mendocino and Lake country wineries.

ALL SEASONS CAFE,
CALISTOGA
3-20-92

## CALIFORNIA WINE COUNTRY RESTAURANTS

There is a freshness and imaginative feeling to restaurants that are near wineries. They are not pretentious. The chefs respect local ingredients and take great pleasure in creating food using seasonal ingredients. Please try to make reservations, as some fill up quickly, especially on weekends. Hours will vary in most of these restaurants. Some are open for lunch on certain days, and some are open for breakfast only on weekends. During certain months some are closed, so please call ahead for current information.

ALL SEASONS CAFE AND WINE SHOP
1400 Lincoln Ave., Calistoga    (707) 942-9111
A cosy and cheery place for lunch or dinner on the main street in Calistoga. There is a wine store in the same room and a lively atmosphere. Sandwiches, pastas and grills are popular here.

## JOHN ASH AND COMPANY
4330 Barnes Rd., Santa Rosa    (707) 527-7687

John Ash is a favorite chef in Northern wine country. His restaurant has high vaulted ceilings, French windows that look out on vineyards, and comfortable chairs for the diners. The menu offers such things as free-range chicken roasted with local greens, and Sonoma lamb laced with thyme and wild honey. The Apple Jack tart and crème brûlée are marvelous. The wine list is extensive. There are prix fixe prices and the 3-course lunch at $14 is certainly a bargain.

## BALLADS,
14220 Hwy. 49, Amador City    (209) 267-5403

This is the dining choice of visitors to the Sierra Foothills wineries. David Funston, from San Francisco's Fog City Diner, creates irresistible dishes. There is a pork tenderloin with tomatillas, jicama and poblano peppers, or veal with panchetta, spinach and gruyère cheese. Prices are moderate and the wine list features the local wineries.

## BRAVA TERRACE
3010 St. Helena Hwy, St. Helena    (707) 963-9300

Fred Halpert, a protege of the late Alain Chapel, has developed a great mixture of American cuisine with French overtones. This is a place where you can drop in for casual or serious dining. There is a version of the French classical dish cassoulet, beautifully prepared fresh fish, and a tasty pork tenderloin. The fresh fruit tarts and crème brûlée are popular here. The wines are well selected and not overpriced.

## CAFE CHAMPAGNE,
32575 Rancho California Road, Temecula,
Culbertson Winery    (714) 699-0088

Cafe Champagne is a most inviting place to enjoy a lunch or dinner after visiting Temecula vineyards. There is seating both on the open terrace and inside. The food is a refreshing California style, which includes mesquite-grilled foods and tasty salads. There is an herb garden beside the restaurant, where the cooks choose fresh herbs each day for their kitchen. The service is friendly. Local wines are featured as well as Culbertson bubbly. Concerts are offered during spring and summer.

## CALISTOGA INN

1250 Lincoln Ave., Calistoga   (707) 942-4101

The Calistoga Inn dining room has a rustic turn-of-the-century atmosphere. The menu is eclectic and the food is delicious. The southwest chicken tamale pie with black bean chili is outstanding. The broccoli rigatoni and chicken divan are also good choices. The wine list is diverse and fairly priced. Breakfasts are hearty and well-cooked.

## COLD SPRING TAVERN

5995 Stage Coach Road, Santa Barbara   (805) 967-0066

Romantic and rustic, this 100-year-old stage coach stop is tucked back in a woodsy hollow. The baked artichoke appetizer is followed by such enticing choices as rabbit with wild mushrooms, excellent steaks, and baby back pork ribs. The servings are generous and dinners include the terrific garlic mashed potatoes. The wine list is excellent. You may want to try a "hobo soda," which is a glass of their famous spring water. There is music in the adjoining bar on the weekends. This is definitely the perfect place to dine after a day of Santa Ynez Valley wine tasting.

## THE DINER

6476 Washington St., Yountville   (707) 944-2626

Breakfast is special here in this warm and cheery diner with its colorful Bauer pottery decoration. Eggs are cooked perfectly, and there are German potato pancakes, huevos rancheros and Jalisco, homemade wheat and sourdough rye breads. At lunch there are some of the valley's best hamburgers and a black bean burrito supremo.

## HI-29 CAFE,

101 Kelly Rd., Vallejo   (707) 224-6303

Recommended by a local for breakfast, this cafe is a winner. It is in a red barn structure and always popular. Breakfasts can be ordered by portions: A is big, B is medium, and C is normal. Pork chops are served with breakfast if desired. Service is quick and friendly. If you are coming or going into Napa, this is a convenient place to stop for a good, filling breakfast.

## KENWOOD RESTAURANT,
9900 Sonoma Hwy., Kenwood

Casual dining among the vineyards. The cuisine is Californian, with some French influence. The Petaluma duck with a fresh orange sauce is one of the best anywhere. A tenderloin of pork is served with sweet and sour red cabbage. There are fresh oysters or steamed mussels for beginnings. A carmelized apple tart or chocolate rum torte is a nice finale.

## MADDALENA'S SAN ANTONIO WINERY
737 Lamar St., Los Angeles    (213) 223-2236

This restaurant, located in the last remaining Los Angeles winery, is popular with the downtown working crowd. You can eat inside, or take your food to the patio across the street. Maddalena's is handy before a downtown concert or theatre. Orders are taken at the counter. The mood is casual, but the food is good Italian home-cooked, and most reasonably priced.

## ORESTES GOLDEN BEAR RESTAURANT
1717 Adobe Cyn. Rd., Kenwood    (707) 833-2327

Tucked away on a 35-acre site in a romantic canyon, you feel miles away from civilization. It is quiet and peaceful, and the Northern Italian cuisine is some of the best in Northern California. The veal piccata is marvelous. The minestrone is the real thing, and the Spumoni is layered and full of genuine ice cream flavors. There is a nice wine list and the service is caring. Brunch on the weekends is popular.

## MADRONA MANOR
1001 Westside Rd., Healdsburg    (707) 433-4231

In this glorious Victorian mansion, award-winning chef Todd Muir prepares some of the most elegant and beautiful creations in the wine country. The sweetbread salad served on a puff pastry, and the asparagus bundles tied with chives, were prepared with caring skill. A perfectly cooked rack of lamb was a joy. The plates are garnished with fresh herbs or flowers from the adjoining gardens. The wine list is excellent and fairly priced. Madrona Manor is the perfect choice for a special occasion.

## MUSTARD'S GRILL

7399 St. Helena Hwy., Napa    (707) 944-2424

Mustard's Grill is the popular choice of Napa Valley.  The menu choices are always exciting.  Some customers order a meal of several appetizers, others the Mongolian pork chop, or calf's liver with carmelized onions.  There is a different soup every day, terrific wines, and it is just a marvelous fun place to be.

## RUSSIAN RIVER VINEYARDS RESTAURANT

5700 Gravenstein Hwy N., Forestville    (707) 887-1562

The Topolos family has taken an 1879 farmhouse and converted the top into a restaurant.  The lower half serves as a tasting room for their Topolos wines.  The menu has many Greek-inspired choices, all with good home-cooked flavors.  The mood is casual, with trees and an herb garden.  This is a relaxing spot and you can taste wine before dining.

## TABLE 29,

4110 St. Helena Hwy., Napa    (707) 224-3300

One of the newest dining places in the valley.  Jonathan Waxman is one of the owners and it shows in the well-balanced menu.  Local ingredients are featured.  A Chenel goat cheese on shaved fennel and arugula is a pleasing combination.  The flank steak with a mound of french fries and onion rings is tasty.  Quail and grills are favorites.  The open kitchen is fun to watch.  David Hockney paintings and other contemporary art decorate the walls.

## TRA VIGNE

1050 Charter Oak Ave., St. Helena    (707) 963-4444

Michael Chiarerro, the executive chef for Tra Vigne, is one of the favorite personalities of the valley restaurant world.  His innovative treatment of Italian cooking is exciting.  There are of course Italian traditional dishes such as pizza and pasta, but these are upgraded and wonderful.  The atmosphere in the lovely stone building is one of the best in the valley.  There is an excellent wine list and terrific desserts.

## TERRA RESTAURANT
1345 Railway Ave., St. Helena    (707) 963-8931

There is a calm Pacific mood to this lovely restaurant, with its attractive stone walls.  Terrific combinations like oysters on a bed of polenta and a very flavorful cioppino are just some of the tasty selections.

## TRE SCALINI,
241 Healdsburg Ave., Healdsburg   (707) 963-5507

If you want some of the best Italian food you have ever tasted, Tre Scalini is the place.  Cynthia and Fernando Urroz, the owners, have a commitment to use only the finest and freshest ingredients, and this is evident in all of their dishes.  The sweetbreads with wild mushrooms are just one of the highlights.  Pasta is served in many fascinating versions, and the homemade spumoni will make you want to return again.  The service and wine list are excellent.

## TRILOGY,
1234 Main St., St. Helena    (707) 963-5507

Tucked in among the store fronts on Main Street, Trilogy offers one of the finest dining experiences in wine country.  Diane Pariseay is a chef with many followers.  In this cosy and calm restaurant you can enjoy a perfectly prepared rack of lamb, lamb with artichokes, or tuna with macadamia nuts and ginger butter.  There is a prix fixe menu.  The wine list offers classics from local vintners.

## VALERIANO'S,
1457 Lincoln, Calistoga  (707) 942-0606

Located in the popular Mount View Hotel, Valeriano's offers excellent Northern Italian cuisine to Calistoga's visitors; pastas, veal, baked artichoke hearts with garlic and parmesan. Desserts include a marvelous homemade ice cream with biscotti and vino santo. Always popular for lunch and dinner.

# INDEX

# INDEX

## BIOGRAPHY

Betty Evans was born in Pasadena, California, and is a third-generation Californian. Betty lives in Hermosa Beach, California, where she is a cooking teacher and food editor of the South Bay EASY READER. In addition to her food interests, she is an honorary docent at the Los Angeles Museum of Natural History, Civic Beautification chairman for the Hermosa Beach Garden Club, and California Collection chairman for the Hermosa Beach Friends of the Library. She is a past Hermosa Beach "Woman of the Year."

Her family, who help in testing recipes, include artist husband Gordon, son Bob (an underwater photographer and inventor living in Santa Barbara), and daughters Suzanne Evans Ackermann (an artist and chef in Zurich) and Jeanne Evans Rosen, a singer and stationery designer in Quartz Hill, California.

CALIFORNIA WINE COUNTRY COOKING is the latest in a popular series that also includes "Honolulu Cooking with Betty Evans", "San Francisco Cooking with Betty Evans", "London Cooking with Betty Evans", "Rome Cooking with Betty Evans", "Paris Cooking with Betty Evans", "Venice Cooking with Betty Evans," and "California Cooking with Betty Evans."

NAPA VALLEY WINE LIBRARY

10-15-91

NAPA VALLEY WINE LIBRARY

## Mail Order Information

Additional COOKING WITH BETTY EVANS books may be ordered from Betty Evans, 1769 Valley Park Avenue, Hermosa Beach, California 90254. Telephone (310) 379-5932.

Make checks payable to Betty Evans. Prices are as quoted below, plus $1.50 (per order) for shipping and handling. California residents add 8% sales tax.

CALIFORNIA COOKING WITH BETTY EVANS   $6.95
VENICE COOKING WITH BETTY EVANS       $6.95
PARIS COOKING WITH BETTY EVANS        $6.95
ROME COOKING WITH BETTY EVANS         $6.95
LONDON COOKING WITH BETTY EVANS       $6.95
SAN FRANCISCO COOKING WITH BETTY EVANS   $6.95
HONOLULU COOKING WITH BETTY EVANS     $6.95
WINE COUNTRY COOKING WITH BETTY EVANS   $7.95

Also available through local bookstores that use the R.R. Bowker Company BOOKS IN PRINT catalogue system. For bookstore discount, order through publisher SUNFLOWER INK.